RON SWORE

1. 5182485 R. A. Beale (Ron) in front of 2 Battalion Gloucestershire Regiment lorry c. 1938, probably at Seaton Barracks, Plymouth.

RON SWORE

The Story of
5182485   Beale R.A.   L/Cpl
2nd Battalion
Gloucestershire Regiment
1935 – 1945

by

NORMAN BEALE
MA MD

2020

THE HOBNOB PRESS

A SLAVE AT TWENTY-TWO

'A slave is someone who is made to work under threat to his life. If a slave tries to run away he is killed. He isn't paid. He is at the will of his masters. It was the same for us. We were given a bowl of soup and some bread made from sawdust. If you didn't do as you were told you were shot. Therefore it was slavery'.[1]

First published in the United Kingdom in 2020

by The Hobnob Press,
8 Lock Warehouse, Severn Road, Gloucester GL1 2GA
www.hobnobpress.co.uk

British Library Cataloguing in Publication Data
A catalogue record for this book is available from the British Library

ISBN 978-1-906978-97-6

Typeset in Scala, 11/14 pt
Typesetting and origination by John Chandler

CONTENTS

PREFACE

FED UP WITH being unable to find work in their home village of *Woolaston, near Lydney, Gloucestershire,* my father and another lad from this very rural community travelled together to Gloucester on Thursday 3 January 1935.[2] They went to the Gloucestershire Regimental Recruiting Centre and asked to join up. Dad had been born in May 1918 and was only 16 years old. Confronted by a recruiting Sergeant he was asked to produce written parental consent, not being old enough to sign on of his own volition (18 years minimum). He had none. Not to be defeated, the Sergeant told him that if he was asked, by the officer taking the swearing-in ceremony, he was to say that he had been born on 20 December 1916 and that he was therefore 18 years old. He was then marched in front of said officer and nudged sharply in the back by the Sergeant when he began to fluff his 'lines'. But, in the end, 'Ron Swore' the oath of allegiance to King and Country to everyone's satisfaction. The 'attestation' form was duly completed and bears his signature just below the false date of birth.

Ron after swearing in and being kitted out and with the unique Gloucestershire Regimental badges, 1935.

During the course of a few seconds Dad had committed himself to seven years' service 'with the colours' and a further five years 'in the reserve'. Within hours he was at *Horfield* Barracks in *Bristol* and 'enjoying' basic training. As a new Private he was posted, in June, to the Second Battalion of the Regiment. Later that year he was sent to *Aldershot* to learn to drive and to acquire some basic motor mechanic skills. It was obviously an intensive course, lasting only three weeks, but he gained a mechanic's qualification and passed the driving test.

Dad (centre, rear) with other members of 2 Battalion Gloucestershire Regiment on the 'sands of the desert'– Egypt 1936

With the Italians threatening British interests in the Middle East, the Battalion sailed to Egypt in January 1936. After a year in the heat and dust of *Mersa Matruh*, 150 miles west of *Alexandria*, it returned to Seaton Barracks in *Plymouth*, arriving on Sunday 2 January 1937. Shortly thereafter Dad became the driver of the Commanding Officer and was made a Lance Corporal. The recorded fact that he was personal chauffeur to the CO has allowed me to follow his movements during the forthcoming actions of the British Expeditionary Force (BEF) in France. It is also the fortuitous circumstance that triggered, indeed provoked, this memoir.

INTRODUCTION

THIS IS A CHIMERA – it combines personal, military and social history, sometimes using other people's prose and pictures. It is dedicated to the International Red Cross and to the *Weinlich/Zajíček* family in the Czech Republic. The reasons for both facts will become clear to the reader. It seemed to me to be the only way to tell the story. Although the book doesn't have the fluency of, say, *War and Peace*, it is about peace, and war and, thankfully, a kind of peace again.

The sanitised and organised stories related by historians must mostly suppress the individual memoire. On the other hand, biography is more intimate. But in this instance the possibility of a straight account with individual and detailed experiences died with the subject 40 years ago. In any case, the person concerned – my father, 'Ron' Beale – would never have participated in the groundwork of a life-story; he would never talk about his experiences. The events recorded here have been gleaned indirectly and many are the general experience rather than that of any individual. Nevertheless, I hope it will be an acceptable record of what happened to my father.

Like so many of his tortured generation Dad had learned to shut out his memories and thereby avoid their consequences. Any acknowledgement of what we now call 'post-traumatic stress disorder' was way in the future in the 1940s and 1950s: locking his emotional wounds into a secure cupboard and throwing away the key was the only tactic then available. Like so many others, Dad paid the price. And so did my Mother, 'Ev' Beale, who had to help him, somehow, struggle through a crisis-ridden period in middle age when the war came back to haunt him. There must be, then, another dedication – to my parents.

METHODOLOGY

THE PERSONAL ELEMENTS of this text are embedded in what I hope to be seen as appropriate and contextual history. This secondary information is extensively referenced and is from published material that is readily available.

My father's individual story has been assembled from his personal papers – his full military service record, his paybooks (which survived his death in 1980) and, amazingly perhaps, the German documentation of his five years as a prisoner of war in Poland. Even more astonishingly, I discovered, in a bundle of ephemera among my mother's effects when she died in 1997, a tiny scrap of paper on which was hand-written the name and address of someone in Czechoslovakia. The only foreign travel either of my parents ever made was by Dad during his military service. Somehow or other, I thought, this surprise finding must relate to that. It reminded me that although Dad was always extremely reluctant to talk about his army years, he had once said that he owed his life to the 'Czech underground' who, at the end of the war, 'got him through to the American lines'. This was very mysterious at the time and he would never elaborate. It has taken many years, and a trip to Poland and to Czechoslovakia where my wife and I met an amazing family, but I can now tell his story. I cannot vouch that it is absolutely correct in every detail since I can no longer obtain corroboration from the central character. Nonetheless I'm confident that it is essentially true, and I hope it will enlighten. Just what was endured without complaint by the ordinary soldiers ('other ranks') during World War Two and, indeed, by their immediate families should not be forgotten.

APOLOGY

THE INEVITABLE MISTAKES I have made must be my responsibility and I hope they will not detract from any remote possibility of 'a good read'. The title of the enterprise might seem odd but the intended pun involves softening the 's' of swore; then all becomes clear, I trust. An apology is owing because I never once heard my father use expletives or blaspheme. However, I wasn't on the scene when, in Lydney, Gloucestershire, where we lived after the war, he once took a sharp left turn out of Newerne Street and the near-side front wheel and suspension of his beloved Morris Minor collapsed and folded the car into the kerb.

I

FROM ONE WORLD WAR TO THE NEXT

At the moment the guns fell silent on the Western Front on 11 November 1918 the British Expeditionary Force was probably the most powerful land fighting force in the world. An Army that had been just 247,000 strong on the opening day of the war, dwarfed by the conscript masses of the other European powers, had expanded fourteen times over. It had grown not just in size but in operational knowledge, confidence and ability.[3]

THE INTENSE AND brutal conflict that had ground to a stalemate of mud and wire in Belgium and France by late 1914 brought about a rapid modernisation of the British Army. By 1918 there was exquisitely accurate ballistic targeting based on aerial reconnaissance, wireless communications and chemical weapons. The individual soldier no longer relied on his rifle and bayonet: there were machine-guns, mortars, grenades and he was able to take advantage of the tank. The upgrading of fighting techniques was phenomenal and all helped to win the war. In parallel, there were rapid and significant improvements in the treatment of the wounded. They were, mostly, rapidly extricated from the line and given immediate surgical stabilisation. But after the war virtually all this military progress in method and in confidence – was lost to expediency.

THE BRITISH ARMY OF THE 1930s

THE BRITISH ARMY in the peace was needed only – or so it seemed – to act as an armed police force around its empire. The massive expansion of the pre-war army was promptly reversed. And after the profound traumas of The Somme and of Passchendaele an act of collective and deliberate amnesia was only human. The surviving regulars were glad, almost, to return to patrolling remote Himalayan borders or manning watch towers in the tropics. But there was another systemic reversion.

Besides shrinking back to former numbers, the post-war army dispersed into its traditional regiments that, though self-sufficient in themselves and renowned for their 'esprit', soon lost all their hard-won ability to coordinate effectively with other units.

Only the British Army regarded the regiment as the essential building block of its organization and identity . . . the regiment mattered. The army did not.[4]

During the next twenty years there were very few occasions when Regiments joined others and practised the arts of fighting in formations such as Divisions or even Brigades. Staff officers were not stretched, logistics and communications untried. To pretend a readiness for war would have been delusional.

If army training was biased towards tasks the troops might undertake in outposts of empire, it was equally skewed by the strong focus on ceremonial duties. Officers of the Gordon Highlanders, for instance, were not passed fit for duty until they had grasped the niceties of their traditional uniforms and were more than competent in highland dance.[5] Having scrupulous table manners and complying with elaborate etiquette were deemed essential for all officers, perhaps because many were not true 'gentlemen' or aristocrats but anxious to be seen as such. In fact, most were middle-class – the sons of service families who, for generations, had provided the state with civil servants, clerics, doctors, teachers and commissioned officers. Life in the army allowed them to live out their fantasies – they could dress smartly, ride to hounds, play status sports, mix with the real 'toffs' and all the while being paid and enjoying privileges such as a 'batman', a personal servant.[6]

'Other ranks', as they were euphemistically called, were from a lower tier of society with no pretence of grandeur. They usually signed on for 12 years – seven with the 'colours' and then a further five in the 'reserve'. Army life, for them, was rough, taxing and communal. They were housed in barracks with shared facilities and up to 30 men slept hugger-mugger on tight rows of iron bedsteads softened only by 'biscuits' – thin mattresses filled with coconut fibre.[7] Their bedding consisted of coarse blankets and their uniforms were made from unforgiving woollen serge. The standard-issue heavy leather boot bearing many steel studs was the nemesis of the infantry, especially when new. Meals were regular but basic – porridge, bread and jam, minced meats, stews, boiled vegetables, perhaps a boiled pudding with custard (often burnt),

Gloucestershire Regiment soldiers cleaning their rifles - late 1930s.
(Randall/Bird family).

semolina and tea; lots of tea.[8] Pay was pathetic – in real value half of what Wellington's men were receiving at the time of Waterloo.[9]

The question of why men were willing to tolerate such poor conditions is, however, easily answered by recalling the socio-economic conditions of the time. In the 1920s, and even more so in the 1930s, after the economic catastrophe of the 'great crash', there was widespread unemployment and grinding poverty. Service life meant comradeship – the Regiment was a surrogate family – and security: men *did* know where the next meal was coming from. They also had the opportunity to learn a useful trade that could be the basis of a later career, be it cook, motor mechanic, telephone technician or one of many other skills. However, recruitment levels fell far short of the peacetime targets even though the process was singularly nonchalant. Teenagers below requisite age often lied about their date of birth and a history of criminality was frequently sanitised, both with the casual complicity of the recruiting Sergeant. The army was the least popular of the three services – the air force was more glamorous, and the navy reputed to be less dangerous. But if the army was the 'Cinderella' service she was still expected to 'go to the ball' and put in a dazzling performance.

THE GERMAN ARMY IN 1939

IT WOULD BE difficult to conceive a greater contrast between the German army of 1939 and its British counterpart. The *'Wehrmacht'* consisted of 116 Divisions (nearly two million men) that were equipped with the latest military hardware[10] while the British had four 'serviceable' Divisions, all short of arms and ammunition.[11] There were, however, other very significant differences irrespective of size and accoutrements even after the small British force was joined to the much larger French army.

After Hitler had been installed as German Chancellor in 1933, he was soon able to eliminate all opposition. With the facility offered to him, as a ruthless dictator unswayed by treaty limitations, he was able to resuscitate the German economy, in part, by initiating a huge drive in production of arms and ammunition, aeroplanes, ships and tanks. The rapid restoration of prosperity generated such a buoyancy in the public mood in Germany that the more sinister aspects of *Nazi* 'reforms' were disregarded by most of the population. The army became a symbol of the new national pride and, in fact, all German society became, somehow, militarised.[12] Young men took it as entirely normal to be called for service when conscription was introduced in

The Wehrmacht had nearly two million men by 1939. (Wikimedia Commons).

1935 (also in contravention to the 1919 peace treaty). Once in uniform, very few questioned the brutal military values they found and there was a communal acceptance that in a new war Germany would prevail and taste victory, if not revenge.

The rape of Poland in the autumn of 1939 did much to normalise inhumanity among the German troops and the so-called *'Waffen SS'* – *Hitler's* storm troopers and nominal bodyguard – were particularly merciless to prisoners of war and innocent civilians alike.[13] The Polish campaign also reinforced the high command's belief in *'Blitzkrieg'* – a lightning war of rapid and disorientating (for the enemy) movement by coordinating air cover and motorised columns of ground troops spearheaded by tanks, all using secure radio traffic.[14] This was the exact opposite of the defensive, stagnant mindset of the French army and, therefore, of the subordinate British Expeditionary Force. Moreover, the Allied air forces considered their role to be entirely in reconnaissance and independent attack.[15]

THE FRENCH ARMY IN 1939

UNLIKE BRITAIN, ITS main ally in World War One, France continued to maintain a very large army after hostilities ceased – nearly 100 Divisions.[16] Colonial obligations aside, the thinking behind such a large commitment was the sanctity of French soil. France had been invaded by Germany twice since 1870 and there was an unshakable desire for it not to happen again. This protective urge led to the construction of a supposedly impenetrable barrier – 'The *Maginot* Line' – along the frontier which stretched from Switzerland in the south to (conceptually) the Channel coast. The French Generals thought only of defence and procrastination; of buying time in the face of an attempted German incursion impaled on their fortifications, time in which they could then devise a strategy to defeat their familiar foe.[17]

By 1939 the French were comfortable with their mass delusion. Their border with Belgium – supposedly an inviolable State – was prone to serious flooding but the water courses were the only possible hindrance to an aggressive invader trampling on Belgian neutrality. The front door might be triple-bolted and alarmed but the scullery window was ajar.

Troops entering the Maginot Line, eastern France, 1940
(Wikimedia Commons. IWM).

PREPARATIONS FOR WAR IN ENGLAND AND FRANCE

HITLER ANNEXED THE *Sudetenland* (German) parts of Czechoslovakia in October 1938 as granted by negotiation. But he proceeded to invade the rest of the country, in defiance of international agreements, within six months. The *'Munich'* compromise allowing British Prime Minister, Chamberlain, to claim 'peace in our time' was dead. Now, with war almost inevitable, the British government upended its policy of resourcing, in the main, its air force and gave new priority to its land forces. Near chaos ensued; giving a starveling a heavy meal can have very unfortunate consequences. The sudden flood of supplies swamped the logistics ability of the army and the abrupt introduction of conscription exposed even more unreadiness. A panicky policy of increasing manpower from four Divisions of regular soldiers to over thirty Divisions using new recruits was a dependable recipe for the mayhem that ensued.[18] And in the middle of this frenzy, senior commanders were briefed by a Cabinet that had been in intense discussions with the French government. A British 'expeditionary force' was to prepare to cross the English Channel immediately on the outbreak of a war. They would be going into a purely defensive role, on the left flank of the French Army, in northeast France.

The *Maginot* Line, constructed by the French during the 1930s, was a multi-layered line of fortifications along the border between France and Germany. The French hoped that it would, for ever, release them from threat of German invasion. However, its northern extremity petered out in the *Ardennes* region where France, Germany, Luxembourg and Belgium meet and where densely forested ravines were thought sufficient barrier. If Germany was going to invade France it would surely do so by crossing Belgium and Holland? 'Tommy Atkins' was going across to help plug this gap in the 'wall'. It was like World War One again. But it wasn't. War had changed – tanks and armoured cars had replaced cavalry; infantry movements were motorised and might have air cover; communications had improved massively. Sadly, this modernisation was rather one-sided and much in favour of the Germans. If the British Expeditionary Force expected to re-enact the fighting of 1914–1918 they were mistaken and, for whatever role, badly equipped. Even for the envisaged task of static defence along the French/Belgian border they would have only a third of the ammunition required and that only for a serious shortfall in heavy weapons such as anti-tank guns. It was also alarmingly obvious that British tanks were much inferior to those of the German army.

A high degree of tactical preparedness based on regular training can overcome deficiencies in arms but there were problems here, too.

'The quality of tactical doctrine and thinking was outmoded and indifferent although there were many excellent officers . . . too many who did not really know their own jobs . . . and whose minds and characters were inadequate for the pace of modern war.'[19]

COMMUNICATION SYSTEMS IN THE ARMIES OF 1939.

THE HIGHLY MOBILE fighting that developed in northern France and the Low Countries after 10 May 1940 put battlefield communications at a premium. In this context, the Germans were found to have a huge advantage over the Allied forces. German signalling techniques were up-to-the-minute and their operators highly proficient. Meanwhile, the French and Belgians and, in particular, the English, were paranoid about their relays being intercepted if they used radios and continued to rely on field telephones and human messengers.[20] This was World War One technology that the Germans had long abandoned: confident that their messages were safely encrypted by the now-famous 'enigma' machines, their units freely communicated by radio. Such highly efficient and immediate ground-to-ground, and ground-to-air, transmissions gave them a very significant advantage in the 'field'.[21] This lead was furthered by the fact that Allied communications often broke down.

Once Allied units had left prepared positions, they were detached from their trusted field-telephone connections and had to rely on civilian channels whose cables were easily damaged in the fighting. Moreover, the civilian staff at telephone exchange buildings were, understandably, reluctant to remain at their posts in the middle of a battle or, indeed, in the middle of the night.[22] This

German battle communications truck 1940 with enigma machine clearly shown. (Wikimedia Commons. Bundesarchiv).

left only the familiar despatch rider on his motorbike or liaison officer in his car. But they too were at risk of interruption – capture if close to military action or serious accidents in panicky traffic on very crowded roads. And if they did find themselves ensnared by a rapidly advancing enemy, the contents of their satchel or briefcase could be of exquisite value to enemy intelligence officers, particularly if written in haste and unenciphered.

British army battle communications early in the second world war - by despatch rider. (Wikimedia Commons. IWM).

2
CONFLICT BEGINS AS 'THE PHONEY WAR'

WE'RE GONNA HANG OUT THE WASHING ON THE SIEGFRIED LINE *

B Y AUGUST 1939 everyone in Britain saw that war with Germany was almost inevitable. No-one was surprised by the announcement, by radio, made by the Prime Minister mid-morning on Sunday 3 September and within hours of the declaration of war, the army units who would be the pioneers of the BEF in France prepared their move. They were regular soldiers who were, it was said, ready for battle. Initially some 150,000 men – infantry, gunners, and their support Companies – assembled at

ports in the Bristol Channel and south coast ports for embarkation. The longer routes to France were selected so that there would be little risk of interception by the *Luftwaffe*. Senior officers did not necessarily wait for their men – there was much staff work to be done in liaison with the French.

The Second Battalion of the Gloucestershire

The British Expeditionary Force embarks for France September/October 1939. (Wikimedia Commons. IWM).

---

* This was a western defensive line built by the Germans during the 1930s. It was parallel, by and large, to the *Maginot* Line of the French and consisted of concrete bunkers, pillboxes, tunnels and 'dragon's teeth' tank traps.

Regiment (2 Glos) was a regular unit under the command of Lieutenant-Colonel the *Hon. Nigel Somerset,* DSO, MC, the great grandson of *Lord Raglan,* commander in chief of the British army in the Crimean War. The Battalion left their barracks in *Plymouth* within a few days of the war beginning and made their way to *Lyme Regis* where the Third Division was assembling. They boarded ships at *Southampton* and arrived at *Cherbourg* on Monday 2 October.[23] The senior officers, however, crossed to Brittany direct from *Plymouth* and, since he was the Commanding Officer's driver, so did Dad, whose paybook shows the party to be in *Brest* on Sunday 1 October.[24]

The BEF was to be commanded by General *John Vereker, 6th Viscount Gort.* A survivor of the previous war, in which he had shown himself to be an extremely courageous officer and winner of the Victoria Cross and other medals for valour, he was seen as being somewhat short of experience as a General and allowing himself to flounder in too much detail.[25] However, as a member of a very old aristocratic family he slotted comfortably into the higher echelons of the class-ridden British Army. More pertinent to the situation, he was resolute, conscientious and popular; clear-headed and decisive. He needed to be – he was in an invidious position. He was leading an army in the field but having to obey strategic decisions from *Paris* and somehow fuse them with tactical orders from *London.* He somehow managed to be compliant and attentive in the face of inevitable contradictions until, after just two weeks of a fighting retreat in May 1940, he was to take a unilateral decision that would save the bulk of his army or, at least, get them back to England to regroup and fight another day.

Lord Gort, Commander in Chief BEF inspects British troops with his French counterpart General Alphonse Georges, early 1940. (Wikimedia Commons. IWM).

Obliged to play second fiddle to the French strategists, the BEF rapidly made its way to that part of the French/Belgian border east of *Lille* that extends from *Halluin* in the north to *Maulde* in the south, a distance of about 40 miles. Their orders were to fortify and man this potential front; to construct what came to be called 'The *Gort* Line', a substitute for the intended *Maginot* fortifications that had never been installed. 2 Glos were billeted in and around the French villages of *Tourmignies* and *Drumez*, south of *Lille* and some 10 miles west of the French/Belgian border that here follows closely the course of the River *Scheldt (Escaut in French)*.[26] They found little that was inspiring or even cheerful. It was 1914 all over again as the men travelled every day across to the border zone and began excavating trenches. The subsoil was heavy clay prone to waterlogging and, worse, full of the detritus of the last war. They unearthed shell cases, rifles, trenching tools,

 steel helmets, gas masks, and personal belongings of all kinds. And the whole area was peppered with unspeakable human remains that had never been given a formal burial. One senior officer even found himself at the billet he had used as a subaltern in the previous war.[27] The men somehow kept cheerful in the face of all these dispiriting reminders of previous conflict even as

The British Expeditionary Force dig in on the French/Belgian border to form 'The Gort Line', early 1940. (Wikimedia Commons. IWM).

they peered across land that was strewn with military cemeteries. The endless rows of white headstones, lovingly tended by the Commonwealth War Graves Commission, seemed, somehow, to be beckoning, one generation to the next.

If the men weren't labouring in water up to their knees, they were training hard for the forthcoming fight. But there was no sense of imminent conflict when beyond the land border in front of them lay only neutral Belgium. There could be no contact with the enemy who was, anyway, fully engaged 800 miles away, in Poland. It was a 'phoney war' or, as one wag named it, *'sitzkrieg'*. As a wet autumn turned into a bitterly cold winter, as 1939 became 1940, so convinced were the Generals that no fighting was looming that the men were even given leave, in rotation, to travel home for 10 days. Dad was given leave in February – he left the front on Friday 2nd and returned to his unit on Wednesday 14th, using his travel warrant to spend a few days in England.[28]

The *Gort* Line followed the France/Belgium border but the lie of the land and some natural obstacles caused deviations and in places it was nearly two miles back into French territory. Encroaching on actual Belgian territory was forbidden for political reasons. Belgian neutrality had to be respected although everyone assumed that this deference would be unheeded by the Germans.

Although the Allied commanders had no wish to repeat the static trench warfare of 1914–18, they had no mandate to attack Germany. A few nocturnal patrols in front of the *Maginot* Line were the sum total of hostilities for over six months. At least there were no serious casualties – bar one very unfortunate British Corporal who triggered a French mine while out on a night patrol on 9 December and was killed. This was the first loss in the BEF and there was sad irony in it being a 'friendly fire' incident – as phoney as the situation itself.[29]

PLAN D

'**B**ATTLE PLAN D' of the Allies had been devised during the first few days of November 1939 at a top-level conference held in a private chateau in *La Ferte-sous-Jouanne*, a small town between *Paris* and *Reims*.[30] In the plush surroundings of the villa, fortified by *'haute cuisine'* meals and expensive wines (chefs had been brought from *Paris*), the delegates were forced to confront the intransigence of their immediate friendly neighbour. Negotiations with the Belgian government had failed to overcome the precondition that Allied forces must not enter Belgian territory for as long as all countries respected the neutrality of its kingdom. Continuing fortification along the Franco-Belgian border therefore seemed the only immediate ploy for the French and British. The Belgians had reluctantly permitted some Allied officers to reconnoitre their territory but secretly and dressed as civilians.[31] The sketchy information gleaned was used to formulate a plan that would be put into play if, and only if, Germany invaded Belgium and ended its neutrality. In this eventuality – which seemed only too likely – Allied forces would immediately move into Belgium and rapidly push east to the line of the River *Dyle* (hence 'Plan D'),* the easternmost of four substantial rivers that transected Belgium, more or less north to south.

* Actually it was more complicated than this – 'Plan E' was the original plan – based on movement only up to the River Escaut but this evolved into the more ambitious 'Plan D' (River Dyle) in the spring of 1940.[32]

It was hoped that any German advance could therefore be stopped on a line between *Antwerp* to the north and *Namur* to the south.

The flaws in the plan were only too obvious. The advancing Allied Divisions would be very prone to air attack by the *Luftwaffe* and on arrival at the *Dyle* they would be attempting to form a front in territory that was entirely unknown to them and with very few established defences. The plan also raised the uncomfortable issue of why so much effort was being wasted in constructing the '*Gort* Line' when it was to be hastily abandoned if and when the Germans invaded Belgium. Figuratively speaking, the concept was one of *La Ferte's* famous millstones hung around the neck of the Allies (millstones had been the main industry in the town for centuries). Nonetheless, the *Dyle* plan was adopted as the best possible scheme in the circumstances. It could, at least, create a narrow front opposite the enemy that was well away from French territory and by protecting *Brussels* it should encourage Belgian troops to fight on.

Lord *Gort* had been involved with the preparation of Plan D but had been a detractor. However, as a subservient commander of a minor force, and after discussing it with *London* and with his subordinates for a couple of days, he felt obliged to accept it. His BEF Divisions were therefore instructed, on 13 November, to prepare for a headlong dash up into Belgium that might come at any time.

THE MECHELEN INCIDENT

GERMANY HAD DEFEATED Poland well before the 1939/40 winter began but not in time to contemplate any major push over its western borders into the Low Countries or France. Nevertheless, *Hitler* began to plan his next move. Expecting stronger opposition than he had found in Poland, a cautious advance through The Netherlands and Belgium seemed the best way to invade and defeat France. This predictable strategy – 'Plan Yellow' – was, to all intents and purposes, a repeat of the so-called '*Schlieffen* Plan' used in 1914.[33] The main thrust of the army would be on the right wing and push through central Belgium with a smaller force providing left wing flank protection to the south, across north-east France. Activity along the *Maginot* Line was seen as diversionary only. There were misgivings in the German high command that this scheme lacked the spark of initiative and surprise but the planning and staff work continued. However, a new plan came with the

New Year: it was a sea change brought about by a critical event.

On Wednesday 10 January 1940 a German aircraft strayed into Belgian airspace whilst flying in dense fog and then developed mechanical trouble. It was forced to crash land near the town of *Vucht* in the Belgian municipality of *Mechelen* (now *Maasmechelen*) close to the German border.[34] Although the *Messerschmitt 108* was irreparably damaged, the pilot and his passenger were unharmed. The passenger, a paratrooper liaison officer, was carrying a copy of the detailed plans for the imminent German invasion. This was totally against regulations and a capital offence of the German military. Not surprisingly he tried to burn the documents retrieved from the wreckage but was interrupted by Belgian police. He made other, frantic, attempts to destroy the papers during the processing of his arrest but only succeeded in drawing attention to their possible importance.

The significance of this major breach in security was not lost on the German high command and an enraged *Hitler* saw that 'heads rolled'. A series of bluffs and counterbluffs then followed after the secret services of both countries became involved but, in essence, one real question remained. Were the documents real or was the information a 'plant'? But whether authentic or not, the documents resulted in Dutch and Belgian troops being put on high alert. Discovering this, and with very heavy snow now falling, the Germans decided to postpone their invasion – tentatively planned for late January.

The longer-term consequence of these events was that *Hitler* demanded a significant change of strategy in order to restore security and regain an element of surprise. It was General *von Mannstein* who promoted a new plan, one which had formerly been dismissed. It turned 'Plan Yellow' on its head. In his revamped 'Plan Yellow' the main thrust (Army Group A) would now be on the left of the invasion, a very strong force of seven armoured Divisions pushing across the rolling countryside of France between *Sedan* in the north and *Reims* in the south. Success would see rapid movement across northern France to the Channel coast between *Calais* and *Dieppe*. A weaker German force (Army Group B) would still invade The Netherlands and Belgium but only in order to entice the French Divisions and the BEF, dug in on the '*Gort* Line', to abandon their defences and move up into Belgium to meet them. Then, within days, the Allies would find themselves encircled by Army Group A and ensnared against the sea. This bold plan had the potential to bring about the surrender of a large section of the French army and the whole of the BEF. In which case, the British Isles would be left virtually undefended. The 'trump card' was the fact that the French had long assumed that German armour could never attack around *Sedan* because it would not be able to penetrate the dense and very hilly hinterland immediately to the north – the forests of the *Ardennes*. This was to prove entirely wrong. The Germans thought they could get through and were prepared to take a necessary gamble, a gamble that was to pay off.

German Plan Yellow ('Fall Gelb'), as revised, for the invasion of France and the Low Countries with the notorious 'sickle cut' by the heavily armoured units of Army Group A after they had sneaked through the Ardennes Forest.

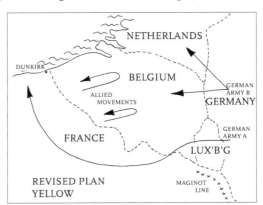

2 GLOSTERS MAN THE MAGINOT LINE

THE 1939/40 WINTER was particularly harsh. Across the exposed, low-lying land where the BEF were hunkered down there was no escape from the intense cold:

The cold went straight through overcoat, battledress, scarves, pullovers, and vests, striking us as if with a sharp knife, into our very bones. Vehicle radiators had to be drained each night to prevent the water freezing . . . bread froze on plates.[35]

Almost worse, and certainly dispiriting, were the intermittent thaws that brought such driving rain that the new earthworks crumbled and collapsed. Digging had to be repeated, whatever the weather.

There was relief, of a sort, for the men of 2 Glos. On Sunday 7 January 1940 they embussed to cross France to the *Saar* region near the city of *Metz* in *Alsace-Lorraine*, some 250 miles to the east.[36] Here there was very deep snow but they had been seconded to man part of the *Maginot* Line and many of the defences were, thankfully, interior.

Otherwise things were less auspicious. Much of *Alsace Lorraine* had been German territory in living memory and many of the locals were native German or German sympathisers. British troops were not welcomed in this part of France. And it was far from reassuring to discover, from personal observation, that the *Maginot* fortifications were often glaringly defective and even missing in places: as a line of defence they were obviously far from dependable.

2 Glos first saw action a week after arriving in the *Saar*. A small patrol, probing forward after dark, heard sounds ahead and suddenly saw a party of Germans approaching through the snow. The patrol leader opened fire and three German soldiers fell, the remainder dispersing.[37] The Glosters then dashed back under covering fire without losses but subsequent night patrols were not so lucky and returned with wounded.

By the time that 2 Glos had returned to their place in the *Gort* Line later in March, there had been a major reorganisation of the units of the BEF. Many of the territorial Battalions that had not been ready for war in September were now fully trained and equipped and had crossed to France. It was thought best to mix these inexperienced Battalions with the more established 'regulars' that had been 'in the field' since early autumn. 2 Glos were now part of the 48th Division (South Midlands) and allocated to 145 Brigade where the other two Battalions (both Territorial units) were the Fourth Battalion of the Oxfordshire and Buckinghamshire Regiment (4 Oxford and Bucks) and the First Battalion of the Buckinghamshire Regiment (1 Bucks). They also found themselves next to familiar cap badges and accents. The 5th Battalion of the Gloucestershire Regiment – also a territorial Battalion – had arrived in France in mid-January and were next to them in the line.[38]

3
REAL WAR

THE GERMANS ATTACK IN THE WEST

JUST BEFORE DAWN on Friday 10 May 1940 the Germans burst through the barriers on their borders with the Netherlands, Belgium and Luxembourg. It was the end of the phoney war. But it had been a true war of a kind – a war of nerves. There had been so many false alarms and panicky moments in the long expectation of a German attack since the previous September that when it really happened there was disbelief and delay. And with immaculately bad timing Belgian soldiers had just been given the news that their leave entitlement was being raised from two days to five days each month.[39]

Within 24 hours many of the Belgian border defenders had been swept aside by German armour coordinating with air cover. The planned blowing of the bridges over many of the large Belgian canals was prevented, in many instances, by lightning strikes of German troops, many of them parachutists. There was much confusion but what was certain was that Belgian neutrality had been defiled. 'Plan D' of the Allies could be put into process and the movement of French and British Divisions into Belgium began on the afternoon of 10 May.

2 Glos had had a disturbed night on 9/10 May. There was anti-aircraft fire around *Lille* aerodrome and the sky had been lit up by searchlights. The reason became known on the seven o'clock BBC news: the Netherlands, Luxembourg and Belgium had been invaded, at dawn, by German troops. *Hitler* had chosen Dad's (true) 22nd birthday to resume the war. As part of 145 Brigade, 2 Glos were ordered to make ready to travel up into Belgium but were held in reserve for four days.[40]

Although the whole world soon knew of the German incursion into The Netherlands and Belgium the *Wehrmacht* was also on the move,

Date.	Place. (If on active Service enter "Field.")	Amount. (State Currency).		Signature and Unit of Officer.
Total from last page				
26/2/40	Field	200		EBernd PSM
28/2/40	Field	200		HA Walter Lieut.
2/3/40	Field	250		
12/3/40	Field	200		capt.
19/4/40	Field	250		capt.
	Field	200		capt.
Total Cash Payments to date ...		1500		
		250		capt.
10/5/40	Field	250		
Total Cash Payments to date ...				

*When a soldier is granted leave to England, an entry stating period of furlough is to be made in second column (i.e., "Place," column).

Paybook of 5182485 R A Beale – comes to an abrupt stop after the entry for 10 May 1940, the day that the Germans invaded Belgium, The Netherlands and Luxembourg.

stealthily, further south. French High Command believed the *Ardennes* impenetrable to German armour but, having crossed into Luxembourg at 04.45 hours on Friday 10 May, it took only a few hours for German motorised units (seven Divisions of tanks and armoured cars) to traverse, virtually unopposed, the narrow defiles of the Luxembourg forests.[41] Strung out, single file, along the few narrow roads and tracks through the forests, they were sitting ducks for any Allied aircraft; but the attacks never came. Now the only natural obstacle to driving south-west onto the plains of northern France was the River *Meuse*. Advance German squads found some of the bridges over the river to be still intact on the afternoon of Sunday 12 May and tried to cross over even while their very demolition was being prepared by French defenders. The Germans were denied and sustained some losses but within 24 hours they had sneaked across mud banks and shallows and had established several significant

bridgeheads south of the river. The weather was fine and continuous *Luftwaffe* bombing and strafing soon demoralised the French Divisions that had been hastily sent to the area. They broke ranks and turned tail before they had even settled into any defendable positions (four of the nine French Battalions sent towards this part of the Belgian *Meuse* never even

Panzers in Ardennes The German army (A Group) stealthily penetrates the Ardennes forest to attack in France, 10 – 12 May 1940. (Wikimedia Commons. Bundesarchiv).

reached the river). The Germans had sent their largest *Panzer* tanks to this front and these were soon being ferried across the *Meuse* and assembling on French territory. By evening of Wednesday 15 May *Panzer* tanks were at *Montcornet*. In other words, the Germans were already west of a north/south line through *Brussels* and *Antwerp* and would storm across northern France to reach the Channel coast in about 10 days. Their '*Sichelschnitt*' (sickle cut) strategy, to give it its nickname, would prove highly effective and had huge consequences for those fighting further north in central Belgium.

Word of a major German breakout into the open countryside of the *Sedan* region reached the French high command on the Belgian front during Wednesday 15 May. On the 16th the French Divisions there, now having an exposed southern flank, were ordered to withdraw. With indications that his ally was retreating, but in the absence of any official information, *Gort* sent a senior liaison officer to French HQ to find out what was happening.⁴² His worst fears were confirmed and he, too, was obliged to order a retreat. Everyone in the BEF was astonished. They had only dug in on the west bank of the *Dyle* a few days before and were holding back the Germans without too much trouble. But

perhaps the enemy was not really trying to do more than hold the Allies in their advanced positions? Many senior British officers had been surprised – and concerned – that their drive up to the River *Dyle* had not provoked any response by the *Luftwaffe*. Could it be that they were being duped by a German strategy and being lured into a noose?⁴³ Was it wise to have abandoned their entrenched positions so casually; to have done exactly as the Germans might have hoped? And now, with the strong possibility of encirclement to the south, they were faced with the horrors of a hasty reversal, all the time being harried from the rear and, now, attacked from the air.

German 'Stuka' dive bomber that was an important component of 'Blitzkrieg'. (Wikimedia Commons).

THE BELGIAN REFUGEE PROBLEM

A T THE VERY beginning of the First World War, soon after the German army had invaded Belgium and northern France in 1914, there were reports of atrocities on civilians. Innocent Belgian citizens were being attacked, physically and sexually, and horrendous stories of personal and property abuse circulated internationally. In particular, the city of *Louvain*, a medieval treasure, was sacked and burned systematically by German troops who appeared to have lost all military discipline.⁴⁴ There were reports of amputations – of hands and even breasts, of gang rape and of random executions, sometimes of whole families. There may well have been embellishments to some of the individual accounts of outrage but among the million or so Belgians who fled their country, 100,000 of them to Britain alone, there were too many consistent stories to allow their dismissal as myth.⁴⁵ In 1940, only 25 years or so later – the span of a single generation – the German army was again rampaging across Belgium from the east. The children of the last war were now parents, their own parents now grandparents: there were too many raw memories for anyone to pretend that they would be unaffected by the invasion. And then, shortly after the event, people began to hear of the carpet bombing of the city of Rotterdam on 14 May and its enormous casualty toll. The urge to flee from the threat of such slaughter from the air and of probable brutality by ground forces, never mind the actual fighting, was overwhelming and a tsunami of humanity was soon surging westward.

Driven by an infectious panic, whole families grabbed what they thought they could carry or push on trolleys or, if middle-class, load into their cars, and formed dense flows of anxious, jostling humankind. By 15 May 1940 the road network of Belgium and northern France was clogged with vehicles, people and abandoned chattels. Eyewitness reports reveal the chaos and the futility:

The roads were streaming with refugees plodding through the night, many of them in carpet slippers, their possessions piled high on rickety perambulators beside which trailed exhausted whimpering children. Aged folk clung for support to the tailboards of overloaded carts to be dragged along, panting, almost faster than their legs could carry them.[46]

The German high command was not going to allow this living flotsam to hinder its advance and had no scruples in reacting violently. There were organised efforts, coordinated by radio communication, to clear the roads ahead of their advance units. The *Luftwaffe* screamed down onto the congested roads and strafed without mercy.[47] Those of the refugees

Long columns of Belgian Refugees and their chattels blocked the roads of their country and of northern France. (Wikimedia Commons. IWM).

who avoided the machine-gun bullets stumbled on but fell silent, listening for the early warning sign of aircraft engines approaching and watching, with every step, for the nearest steep embankment or, better still, ditch. The British and French army units had no means of avoiding their becoming snarled up in the exodus and of being marooned in the many stagnant queues. Their progress across what was a very mobile battlefield was hopelessly hindered, even at night.

4
2 GLOSTERS MOVE UP INTO BELGIUM

Tuesday 14 May 1940

BY EARLY AFTERNOON everyone in 145 Brigade was well prepared to move and 2 Glos led the way.* The first part of the journey from *Tourmignies* – through *Tournai* and *Ath* – was uneventful and low key: the ecstatic citizens, cheering and lobbing gifts, that had greeted units moving up over the weekend had been replaced by disconsolate civilians and small groups of Belgian troops heading west. The Brigade column received some unwanted attention, however. It was bombed on the outskirts of *Enghien* but without sustaining any damage. The *Luftwaffe* attacked again while the Brigade was stuck in heavy traffic in *Halle* but again without harm.

10 – 15 May 1940 – The BEF moves up into Belgium to confront the German Army (B Group). (Wikimedia Commons. IWM).

The bulk of the Brigade was south of *Brussels* by 1600 hours. Although there was a lot of air activity and anti-aircraft fire everyone eventually arrived at their rendezvous. For 2 Glos this was in woods south of *Alsemberg* and an advance party, finding no signs of the enemy, had evicted remaining civilians from nearby villages to provide billets.

* The following detailed record of the movements and battles of the Second Battalion, Gloucestershire Regiment (as part of 145 Brigade) during the period 14 May to 31 May 1940 are compiled here from the three personal daily recollections (when prisoners of war) of Lt. Col. N F Somerset (later Brigadier), of Major E M B Gilmore (later Lt. Col.), and of Capt. H C W Wilson. Gloucestershire Regimental Museum Archive, Gloucester.

Wednesday 15 May 1940

THE BRIGADE WAS all woken by a flight of German bombers that came very low over the area at 0500 hours but this was intent on another target. Small arms fire was ineffective other than in wakening everyone. *Somerset* and his Company commanders joined the Brigadier and they travelled to a staff conference near *Waterloo* village. *Somerset* and his Adjutant went on to tour the area around the *Waterloo* battlefield later that morning, trying to identify suitable natural defensive positions. It was the very ground where his great grandfather, Lord *Raglan*, had fought with *Wellington* at the Battle of *Waterloo* in 1815. However, there was no time for reminiscence. The Germans had kept up their bombing and strafing and the passengers of the staff car, with their driver, had to dive for cover on one occasion.

On his return, about 1400 hours, the Brigadier (*Hughes*) announced that he was ill, that he had been told to leave at once, and that *Somerset* was to take over command of the Brigade. 2 Glos was hastily reorganised; Major *Gilmore* taking over as Commanding Officer of the Battalion. Presumably Dad now became *Gilmore's* driver, *Somerset* inheriting all the support staff of Brigade HQ. At 1830 hours there was firing from suspected fifth columnists and a party from HQ company was sent out to 'round them up'. Two were shot outright by a Belgian liaison officer.

Before having any opportunity to settle himself into his new responsibilities, *Somerset* was ordered to take the Brigade further forward to the River *Dyle* 'line' between *Wavre* and *Namur* and relieve a French (Moroccan) Division that had given way to the enemy to the south-east of *Waterloo*. After all the necessary reorganisation the Brigade marched off at 2200 hours leaving transport in the protection of the *Alsemberg* woods. Whilst on the march new orders arrived – that the Brigade make for Waterloo and establish new Brigade HQ there.

Thursday 16 May 1940.

SOME OF THE men lost their way in the dark and it was 12 hours before they were in their positions, 2 Glos initially in the area around the village of *Joli-Bois*, just north of the old *Waterloo* battlefield. Retreating Moroccan troops were passing through the village all afternoon and then, during the evening, an increasing crush of civilian refugees.

In touring the new positions, the staff officers had to run for the cover of a building when German planes came in low using their machine-guns. There were other air attacks on many of the positions and *Somerset* was increasingly apprehensive – his men were widely stretched and there were no apparent links to other units on either flank. There was an eerie absence of enemy ground troops even though the Brigade was very close to where the Moroccans had given way.

In attending another conference at Division HQ, *Somerset* learned of the German breakthrough near *Sedan*. Although this was some 120 miles to the south it carried the obvious threat that Allied troops presently in central Belgium could be encircled from the rear. The whole BEF was to retreat westwards immediately.

145 Brigade was told to begin their withdraw under cover of dark – at 0200 hours (17 May) - all transport having been sent back earlier, and to march across country with weapons. 2 Glos were the rearguard and, after a series of false alarms during the evening, found themselves in a firefight with the enemy when passing *Waterloo* itself. There was no way this was ever going to be seen as the second Battle of Waterloo and, thankfully, no casualties were reported. Marching continued all night: it was the beginning of a long and exhausting retreat.

5
2 GLOSTERS JOIN THE RETREAT FROM BELGIUM

Friday 17 May 1940

2 GLOS WERE still marching westward when dawn came. It was the beginning of a day in which the Companies were repeatedly attacked from the air, and in making their way towards *Halle* they marched in single file along the road margins, always ready to dive into hedges or ditches. If possible, they snaked through woodland or cross-country using compass directions. By evening the Companies were back together at *Enghien* but though food was available there was no rest, even though they had marched nearly 30 miles in 18 hours carrying rifles, Bren guns and anti-tank weapons.

Orders had arrived that the Brigade was to form an immediate defensive line to the west of *Enghien* and be on alert all night. The Companies dispersed and prepared for an expected attack. They soon came under a heavy bombardment but the Germans seemed to concentrate on the town itself except for some shells that landed very near Brigade HQ.

Saturday 18 May 1940

2 GLOS COMMANDING Officer, *Gilmore*, was woken at 0400 hours with orders to report,

The BEF try to stop the German advance across Belgium while having to retreat every night. (Wikimedia Commons. IWM).

immediately, to Brigade HQ for a conference. He and his driver set off with the directions given but Brigade HQ could not be found. They returned in full daylight and to the sounds of battle in *Enghien* to find orders for a full and immediate withdrawal of the Brigade to beyond the River *Dendre* at *Ath*, 2 Glos acting as rearguard. Everyone was away by 0730 hours and could see how badly *Enghien* had been bombed overnight. The enemy was certainly now following very close behind the general retreat. The main road west to *Ath* is straight and exposed, and armoured cars, acting as outlying protection, fought off German armour at one point when it appeared from the southeast. 2 Glos CO and a reconnaissance unit drove on ahead to scout positions and possible billets at *Ath*. The men were having to march through their tiredness and it didn't help that they had to wear their respirators during the hottest part of the day after a gas alarm (false). Decades later the men could well remember the extent of their fatigue:

We was getting no sleep and we was absolutely exhausted . . . we was sleeping on the march, walking automatically, and the next minute you would bump into the person in front because you didn't realise they had stopped. You just lost track of time and feeling. If it was a rest break, you'd be down on the ground right away, taking as much rest as you could. But once it came to getting up again, it was quite a struggle. You were bullied into getting up.[48]

Otherwise the Brigade was lucky and no air attacks came in. The 15 miles to *Ath* were covered by about 1600 hours but there was no universal rest on arrival. 2 Glos detachments were sent off to protect Royal Engineer units preparing to blow all the bridges over the *Dendre*, timed for 2000 hours. Many were able to see several large German planes (probably carrying troops) come in very low over *Ath*, and before long there was incoming mortar fire across the area. Finally, the Brigade could all settle to a small meal (food was getting very short) at their bivouacs in a wood to the west of the town. At Brigade HQ, however, a liaison officer had just arrived with orders for withdrawal to *Maulde*, south of *Tournai*, beyond the next major river, the *Scheldt (Escaut* in French). The Brigade was to leave at 0300 hours and rendezvous with motorised transport around 0500 hours.

Sunday 19 May 1940

THERE WAS INTERMITTENT firing all night and a small 2 Glos detachment led by a 2nd Lieutenant did not return from a night patrol. There was no time to investigate before leaving and these men were the first losses of the Battalion bar one case of acute appendicitis earlier evacuated to England. The Battalion easily reached the main road from *Ath* to *Tournai* but here they found serious congestion. They became entangled with men and vehicles from several other Brigades and fragmented units. There was no transport waiting for them at the designated location so they were forced to march on, still carrying rifles and some heavier weapons. Eventually buses began to appear, in ones or twos. They were a cheering sight, quickly turned around and loaded. The Companies shared them. They were then driven off at speed towards *Tournai* – daylight was imminent and with it the risk of air attack. Just after passing through *Leuze*, however, and looking to turn south, the buses ran into a very dense traffic jam. There were vehicles of all kinds, civilian and military, head to tail and three to four abreast. Yet more vehicles were edging their way in from side roads. Military police were trying to organise priority for army units and one or two of the buses with 2 Glos men on board managed to squeeze through the jam but then missed the turning going south to *Antoing*, the agreed route to *Maulde*.

Then the inevitable happened. Nine Heinkel German bombers came along the line of the road and bombed the traffic, the buses with some of 2 Glos aboard mixed in with it. Some men managed to jump out of their transport but could find no cover as they watched the German planes bank around and return, firing their machine-guns. Some vehicles were hit directly by bombs and everyone still on board was killed outright or burned alive in the resulting inferno. An ammunition truck was hit, creating yet more casualties, and many men were cut down by the hail of bullets on second pass of the planes. About 130 men from 2 Glos were unaccounted for when some sort of order was restored. It was the worst loss to Luftwaffe attack on the BEF throughout the campaign.[49] The CO, *Gilmore*, and his Adjutant had been towards the back of the column in a staff car (presumably driven by Dad) and were also targeted. The Adjutant was wounded and later evacuated to England. He survived and wrote of this experience:

'It was just getting light when we arrived on the outskirts of Tournai. Here there was a terrible congestion of traffic, which reminded one of the traffic one sees going to an important race meeting. Cars were four abreast and mixed up with numbers of refugees. I saw nine bombers at low level coming over our positions and had just decided that they were enemy aeroplanes and ordered the Anti-aircraft Bren in the truck behind me to fire, when the bombs started falling. This was followed by machine gun fire. An ammunition truck went up near me and bombs seemed to explode on part of 'A' company who were just behind me. About 70 of A and HQ Companies were killed, wounded or missing in this raid. I was the only officer wounded and got two bits of bomb in my body.[50]

Along two to three hundred metres of road there were dead, dying and wounded everywhere, some badly burned and some with bullet or shrapnel wounds, soldiers and civilians alike; men, women and children in the latter instance. The cremated remains of the men in the buses and other burning vehicles were an indescribable horror. Private Bill Lacey of 2 Glos recalled the incident when interviewed for a television programme that was broadcast in 2005:

There wasn't much left of the convoy but they started shouting to us to get back on. There was bodies all over the place at the time. There were two bren-gunners, still hanging on to their guns, and they were obviously dead. There were arms and legs in different places, and it was more like a rubbish heap, spread all over the place. There were stretcher-bearers working but they couldn't cope because they were just picking up limbs.[51]

It was over two hours before the situation was under control and the remaining Glosters could rally themselves and resume their journey. Then, later in the day, the CO heard of further losses – the buses that had missed the turning to *Maulde* had been bombed on the outskirts of *Tournai*. An officious sapper Major had insisted on lining up all the military vehicles in a tight queue and so offered a perfect target for the German bombers.[52] Several dozen more men from 2 Glos had been killed. After a brief respite during the late afternoon 2 Glos were arranged into defensive positions on the west bank of the *Escaut (Scheldt)* close to the villages of *Hollain* and *Jollain-Merlin*, five miles north of *Maulde*, their original day's destination.

At evening rollcall, it was found that nearly 300 men were missing from the whole Brigade. Some were astray and turned up later, but most were dead or wounded: it was the most grievous loss so far. Many in the Battalions would have been thinking of lost friends that night. When told that if the enemy managed to cross the river they were to stand and fight there was actually great relief among the men – anything would be better than more retreating, especially if on foot. In fact, the night was quiet and most got some rest, in shifts – the first for five nights.

6
2 GLOSTERS DEFEND THE ESCAUT LINE

Monday 20 May 1940

THE 2 GLOS POSITIONS were consolidated from early morning and the CO went around making an inspection. He found Companies well dug in and having a good view and lines of fire to the far bank of the *Escaut* where there was a lot of open ground bar one small copse. Gilmore re-inspected the positions in early afternoon when he showed round the acting Brigadier. Somerset must have felt very much at home among 'his' men. And, on returning to his HQ, he found a teleprint from Lord *Gort* confirming his promotion to Brigadier and his command of 145 Brigade.

The enemy attacked at about 1500 hours, starting up a heavy bombardment. Constant infantry movement was seen across the river and enemy platoons made repeated attempt to cross under cover of the artillery fire. A stream of reports arrived at Brigade HQ that Gloster Companies were intensely engaged in fending off attacks. The enemy failed to cross the river on the Gloster front but there was no doubt that they were now following the BEF closely and that they had very aggressive intent. By mid-evening the bombardment had subsided but small arms and machine-gun fire continued until well after dark. Everyone was very tired but the men were pleased to have found that they had the resolve and ability to hold back the enemy if given the opportunity.

Tuesday 21 May 1940

THE GERMANS WERE now well-established on the far side of the River *Escaut* opposite the Gloster Companies. They were sending mortar and shell fire into 2 Glos positions nearly all day but fortunately there were no casualties. Less comforting was the news that the enemy had managed to cross the river in force a mile or two further north. C Company adjusted their posture to watch for enemy approach on their left flank, but none came. In fact, other reports came in that the incursion was only a rumour. No-one seemed sure whether the threat was real or not, but the Germans were certainly going to get across sooner or later. Although there was a lull in the afternoon, aggressive firing from the far bank resumed early evening. It was therefore dark before it was safe for transport to bring forward food and supplies and everyone enjoyed a hot meal at midnight. There were periods of machine-gun and rifle fire throughout a very disturbed night.

Wednesday 22 May 1940

THE CO VISITED the Companies at 0800 hours and found them cheerful and well ensconced. They were taking it in turns to get some sleep in their foxholes. Mid-morning a German spotter plane flew low over positions and during the afternoon Battalion HQ received some very accurate shelling. It was felt wise to move the HQ together with the neighbouring Regimental Aid Post. The actual move, though, was prevented when a very intense enemy bombardment began about 1700 hours and continued all evening. It was ineffectual however; the men held their positions safely and enemy infantry approaching the opposite riverbank were turned back, after sustaining losses, by accurate rifle and machine-gun fire. A report came in, however, that the Germans had, now, definitely, advanced beyond the *Escaut* just south of *Tournai*. Then, about 2300 hours, came an order for a complete and immediate withdrawal of the Brigade, hopefully after a smooth disengagement from the enemy.

Thursday 23 May 1940

MEASURES TO DISGUISE the withdrawal of the Companies from the enemy were successful and by 0200 hours the CO and the Adjutant, last to leave, were driven away into a mist. They had some difficulty finding their way but caught up with the Brigade just as they were completing their seven-mile night march to *Rumegies*, to the southwest of *Hollain*. It was getting light as the columns arrived. After their eight-day foray into Belgium they were now back in France.

They were therefore able to see the 'Gort Line' defences they had helped to prepare during the autumn and note, with some annoyance, and anxiety, that the line was completely unmanned. Had all their efforts been a complete waste of time? In fact, everyone was too tired to care very much.

BEF France 1940 – Officers' briefing on next move for their unit. The desperate retreat across Belgium and to the channel ports for fear of being surrounded was inevitably hectic and confused. (Wikimedia Commons. IWM).

The 4 Oxford and Bucks were placed along the actual fortification and 2 Glos moved back as reserve, around the villages of *Rumegies* and *Sameon*, Battalion HQ in the former. Everyone now managed to get some sleep, for although there were the sounds of bombing and artillery all day, none of it was close by and there was no approach of the enemy. Some rest was very necessary – there was to be yet another night march starting late that evening. A sequence of orders had come in, all different, but the last of them was that the Brigade was to move further west – to the village of *Nomain*, to within three miles of where the men had started their fateful journey into Belgium. Other news had also arrived at Brigade HQ – that the *Panzer* Divisions of German Army Group A were rapidly closing on the Channel coast near *Abbeville*. The BEF was facing the possibility that it was in the middle of a pincer movement.

REALITY DAWNS AT BEF HQ

THE INCREASINGLY SERIOUS situation in France and the Low Countries marked by the spectacular advance of the *Panzer* Divisions of German Army Group A and the increasing chaos of the Allied retreat across Belgium provoked urgent meetings in Whitehall. The new Prime Minister, *Winston Churchill*, only a week in office, was told that it seemed more and more likely that the BEF would have to be ferried back across the English Channel. Securing at least one continental channel port and assembling a fleet of ships in southeast English ports were more necessity than insurance. All this fell under a very strong spotlight when, on Monday 20 May, a jubilant enemy *Panzer* Division roared into *Abbeville*, only a few miles from the Channel coast.[53] If the Germans now turned north (as they did) the BEF would be encircled.

But in France plans were still being made, jointly between BEF staff officers and their French overlords, to take the initiative.[54] The notion was to send a large armoured force south towards *Arras* and to cut through the German columns that were passing east to west and so isolate their spearhead. Battle orders were completed early in the week beginning Monday 20 May and involved two British Divisions manoeuvring into position alongside three of the French. They faced enormous difficulties, however. Many roads were heavily congested and travelling along them by day risked aerial attack by the *Luftwaffe*. The logistics support was virtually non-existent – ammunition, fuel, provisions and reserve troops were not where they would be needed and as the week progressed commands from French HQ were repeatedly amended and were often contradictory.

Lord *Gort* was very unhappy with the overall situation, even more so as reports of a collapse of the Belgian army reached him. By mid-week *Calais* was virtually surrounded[55] and if the Belgians really were giving up the fight on the coastal flank of the retreat through their country the Germans could be racing towards *Dunkirk* from the east within a few hours. Protecting his only remaining port for reinforcement from England was surely more important than launching a risky counterattack? *Gort* wrestled with this dilemma and whether or not he had the power to act independently of the French command for a couple of days. But by the week's end he was determined; his best purpose was to save his army from entrapment by turning it northwards towards

Dunkirk,* hopefully within the protection of a secure corridor.[56] He also had the comfort of knowing that preparations for a possible escape by sea were already in hand at *Dover.*[57]

It was obvious to *Gort* that he had insufficient time and too small a force to set up a coherent defensive line across the enemy advance, which was now from the east, from the south and, increasingly, from the southwest. There was an imminent danger of total encirclement and the capitulation of what was virtually the whole of the serviceable British land forces. It was easily possible that the spearhead of the German Army Group A, already at *Calais,* would soon cut off access to all the Channel ports and any possible means of escape. The only hope was to harass and fragment the German onslaught by setting up defensive 'strong-points'.[58] Each location might soon be surrounded and overrun but this desolate tactic, forlorn for the detachments involved, could buy some time. A mere day or two could allow significantly more of his other retreating troops to struggle up his perception of an 'escape corridor' to the coastal area around *Dunkirk,* the only port that might still be available (see map). And perhaps *Dunkirk* could then be held

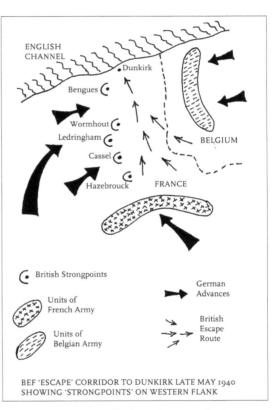

BEF 'ESCAPE' CORRIDOR TO DUNKIRK LATE MAY 1940
SHOWING 'STRONGPOINTS' ON WESTERN FLANK

*   In fact Gort took his final decision to drop all plans for British elements to be part of any retaliatory breakout against the Germans on Saturday 25 May. And by that weekend he had also agreed with London that wholesale evacuation from Dunkirk should begin (non-combatants and wounded had actually been leaving for several days).[59] A sequence of resistant strong-points some 20 miles out from the port were, in the end, to serve only to cover the escape of the bulk of the British Army but those out in the line weren't to know this for another three or four days, if ever.

for long enough to embark at least some of the expeditionary force and get them back to England. Partial repatriation now appeared to be the only alternative to a rout, but could it be organised? And was it possible? Reaching the sea was only the first of many hurdles.

 Gort then learned, from an intercepted German signal, on Friday 24 May,[60] that the enemy were under orders to halt their armoured advance – now approaching from the southwest – and he took the opportunity to form his defensive line of strongpoints through *Wormhout, Cassel* and *Hazebrouck* (see map). He only had sufficient troops to man the main towns themselves (the western aspect of his 'corridor' to the sea) but he hoped that such 'strongpoints' might just break up and delay the German advance long enough to allow the bulk of the British Expeditionary Force to reach *Dunkirk*. If the isolated 'stops' could hold out for two or three days it might just be sufficient time for the rest of the British to retreat to inside a ring of more substantial defences formed around the inland margins of *Dunkirk* – land that was full of watercourses and not ideal tank country. This was the strategic concept behind new orders that were to be sent to 145 Brigade during the afternoon of Friday 24 May and Brigadier *Nigel Somerset*, though newly promoted only a few days earlier, was to be a key figure in this part of the plan.

Friday 24 May 1940

EVERYONE IN 145 BRIGADE must have been very relieved to find the town of *Nomain* deserted as they entered the community early morning of 24 May. There were plenty of places to sleep and there was the prospect of a full day's rest. But at 0700 hours new orders arrived from Division HQ. *Somerset* was to take his Brigade to *Calais* to relieve what was now a siege of the town. The brief included the promise of road transport – *Calais* was, after all, 100 miles to the north – but none arrived. The men got their rest after all and by the afternoon of what was a beautiful summer's day there was something of a party atmosphere. Some of the men had hijacked a piano and a singsong had been organised. The officers were enjoying a picnic in the sun.[61] The war seemed a long way off before the euphoria was punctured by yet more orders:

You are to proceed to Cassel. We do not know where the enemy are, but we hope you will get there first . . . troop transports will arrive this evening.[62]

Now, it seemed, they were being sent to somewhere called *Cassel* and maps were rapidly consulted. *Cassel* was 50 miles northwest – through *Lille* and *Armentieres*. From latest reports this was a heading that would take them towards the present whereabouts of the German *Panzer* spearhead. Motorised transport was again part of the plan and this time it arrived.

Despite being on the move *Somerset* received a clear radio message in the middle of the night. He was ordered to send one of his three Battalions to *Hazebrouck*, some nine miles to the south of *Cassel*. *Hazebrouck* had also been selected as one of *Gort*'s 'strongpoints' and because they were at the back of the columns, *Somerset* diverted 1 Bucks, he himself spending some time at a crossroads to direct them and give them their orders. He then re-joined his truncated Brigade which now consisted of two infantry Battalions – 2 Glos and 4 Oxford and Bucks together with a few tanks, 10 Bren gun carriers, a few machine-gun squads, and some 18 lb guns and crews from an assortment of Armoured Brigades.

7
2 GLOSTERS ARRIVAL AT AND DEFENCE OF CASSEL 25 – 29 MAY 1940

Saturday 25 May 1940

THE REMAINING TWO-THIRDS of the Brigade approached *Cassel* in what was, by now, full daylight. The mass of the hill on which the town sits could be seen rising out of the otherwise totally flat Flanders plain. Their destination was a welcome sight – moving columns of vehicles were a tempting target for the *Luftwaffe*, as the men well knew and, as if to remind them, there were scattered corpses of refugees alongside the roads where they had been bombed and strafed by the Germans. Thankfully, the Brigade was not molested from the air despite the morning being fine and clear. But were the enemy ground troops already in the town? It was entirely possible. The Brigade chaplain, *David Wild*, found himself ahead of the fighting troops and reported his apprehension:

. . . for all I knew we were driving straight towards the enemy (but). . . we were a little cheered to see some of our artillery in position to the left of the road some two miles from Cassel. Evidently the Germans had not arrived.[63]

However, the town itself was already badly damaged and there were some gruesome signs of enemy bombing:

The last long climb follows a series of zigzags up the steep face of the hill until the road takes a sharp right-angle bend straight into the narrow main street. The corner was not a cheering sight. Some French . . . horse-drawn artillery had taken a direct hit at this point, and all over the road were scattered the remains of wagons, guns, horses and men.[64]

From that moment the spot where this carnage had taken place was invariably referred to by the British soldiers as 'Dead Horse Corner'. There were also burnt-out vehicles in the main square – the *Grand Place'* – and several buildings were already just heaps of masonry. *Wild* was very reassured, though, to see British officers and men moving purposefully around the town and to find several Bren-gun carriers parked in the square.

The town of *Cassel* had been, already, the scene of many battles even back to Roman times. It was said to be the location of the nursery rhyme in which the 'Grand Old Duke of York' had marched his men 'up the hill' and then 'down again', but this has been disputed. It was certainly, though, home to General *Foch's* headquarters during the First World War. The reason for its strategic significance is easily understood. The town is perched atop an isolated hill that rises to about 500 feet above the surrounding plain, giving an uninterrupted view of many square miles of countryside in most directions. There is, though, immediately to its east and linked by a neck of land, a subsidiary hill; the *'Mont des Recollets'*. This prominence is wooded and virtually uninhabited. *Cassel* itself, however, is also a vital road junction. Important roads lead south-east – to *Lille*; south – (eventually) to *Amiens*; south-west – to *St.Omer* and thence to *Calais*; and north – to *Dunkirk* (which is easily visible on this horizon). The Allied High Command was very well aware of the strategic potential of the town, being familiar with its unique situation. The habitation of the town surrounds a central *'place'* or square. There is an ancient chateau, a large *'Hotel de Ville'* and the usual dwelling houses, shops, banks and offices. Various lanes lead down between the houses and there are many walled gardens on the slopes of the hill. In 1940 there were some 2000 inhabitants. Many, but not all, had fled; the town already having been bombarded and strafed from the air by the Germans.

The Brigadier himself arrived in the town at 0600 hours and, in taking over command, was briefed by Major-General *Mason-MacFarlane* who was in charge of a mixed force of light tanks, armoured cars, anti-aircraft guns and some searchlight platoons. These were all being withdrawn to the coast with immediate effect. The orders *Somerset* received were very simple. His Brigade was to hold *Cassel* 'at all costs'. This time there was to be no pulling back. 'The safety of the BEF depends on us' *Somerset* was to tell his staff, and they well understood the implications of that familiar phrase: 'last man, last round'.[65]

The town was seen as part of a punctuated perimeter to protect *Dunkirk* – the last Channel port available to the Allies for the purpose of reinforcement from England and from which to launch a breakout (at least, this is what *Somerset* and everyone in 145 Brigade understood at the time). In terms of frontage, 145 Brigade – 'Somerforce' – had orders to hold a line between a blockhouse two miles north of Cassel on the road to *Dunkirk* through Cassel itself, to *Hondeghem* and on to *Hazebrouck*, nine miles to the south.

To hold a front of 11 miles would be a considerable challenge for a full Brigade but 'Somerforce' was already considerably under-strength. The men were tired, hungry and their numbers depleted, even if the residue of the force made it to the town. *Somerset* recognised that it was of no use to make a highly co-ordinated plan of defence – the distances were too great. If the Germans attacked between the various defended villages and towns there was nothing to stop them: it was no use scattering infantry over what was excellent tank terrain. Like Gort, he had to hope that the enemy could be delayed in its advance on *Dunkirk* by fortifying and tank-proofing the towns he had been allocated. It was obvious that *Cassel* was best-situated in this respect.

Mason-McFarlane also briefed the Brigadier on recent enemy activity in the area. *Cassel* had been heavily bombed the day before and a French Transport unit, much of it horse-drawn, had been caught in the town, sustaining heavy casualties, many of which still lay unattended. Enemy armoured cars had also approached the town in recent hours, shot up in various directions and then driven off. *Mason-McFarlane's* own armoured vehicles had, for some days, been in contact with the enemy to the southwest of the town, near the *Bois de Clairmarais* some five miles distant: they had suffered significantly when they found themselves against heavy tanks. The German armoured thrust across France from east to west had obviously now turned to drive north hoping to encircle the BEF and the French First Army.

The Brigadier made an immediate brief recce around *Cassel:*

' . . . *as I wanted to get the troops dispersed and under cover in case of further air raids.*'[66]

He decided to send the arriving 2 Glos Battalion to occupy the northern and western parts of the town, while 4 Oxford and Bucks Battalion would occupy the southern and eastern sectors (see map p. 52). The Ox and Bucks would also detail a Company for 'The Keep', which was a building on higher ground in the centre of the town. Here there were good cellars and cover generally and it would be possible to hold out for a considerable time given the necessary ammunition, food, water, etc. 4 Ox and Bucks were also given the defence of the *Mont des Recollets,* where some light tanks were bivouacked (but left later that day).

It was about 0800 hours when trailing elements of 2 Glos drove up the eastern approach road to Cassel and on assembly it was obvious that considerable numbers were missing. 2 Glos CO, Major *Gilmore,* directed the transports to the side of the road under the cover of trees. Then, leaving the Adjutant in charge, he was driven up into the town itself to try to find the Brigadier and receive orders regarding the disposition of his troops.

The first task facing the members of 145 Brigade as they arrived in *Cassel* that Saturday morning was to turn the town into a tank-proof fortress. The main threat was expected to come from tanks so that all artillery was sited and set for anti-tank roles. Roadblocks were begun on all main roads leading into the town and covered by the battery of guns allocated to the force. The walls of buildings around the outer limit of the town were loop-holed, and roofs and ceilings were shored up, until the whole town was converted into a kind of fortress. Some of this work provoked angry protests from local inhabitants. They had been ordered to leave the town but many of them had simply scurried into cellars where they were hiding in the hope that the war would wash over them and leave everything intact. This was not to be and there were suspicions that resentful locals became fifth columnists inclined to help the Germans push out the destructive *Anglais.*

Machine-gun nests were set up and the 18-pounder guns of the Royal Field Artillery units installed at promising positions. *Somerset* also made an urgent request to GHQ for some 25-pounder guns to be diverted to the town so that the *Bois de Clairmarais* would be in range. But, like the anti-aircraft units he also requested, they were never to materialise. Some Royal Engineers that did arrive in the town he set to directing the construction of the roadblocks and other barricades once it was clear that all his force had arrived (which, it transpired, was not until well after midday).

The Brigadier set up his HQ in the Chateau just north of the main square in the town and 2 Glos made their HQ in the town bank, and bank manager's house adjoining, in the town square. Within hours it was moved below ground into two adjoining cellars and the dividing wall was loop-holed. The Regimental Aid Post was established in the next house along the square.

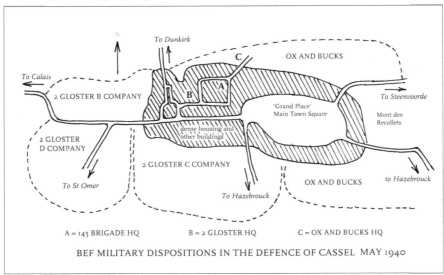

A = 145 BRIGADE HQ   B = 2 GLOSTER HQ   C = OX AND BUCKS HQ

BEF MILITARY DISPOSITIONS IN THE DEFENCE OF CASSEL MAY 1940

At 1500 hours Brigadier *Somerset* made a detailed recce of 2 Glos sector with the Commanding Officer of the Battalion, Major *Gilmore*, taking the Commanders of the Royal Artillery and Royal Engineers units with them. As there were so many civilians about, *Somerset* decided to order them all out of the town and asked the French liaison officer to do this. However, there were so many cellars in the place that hundreds of people remained behind, living in unbelievable filth and stench.

By the evening a great pall of smoke could be seen due north – where *Dunkirk* was burning and, after dark, it was obvious that the coastal town was extensively on fire. But in *Cassel* the officers and men had, for once, a peaceful night's sleep after plenty to eat from the abandoned houses and shops.

Sunday 26 May 1940

A T 0900 HOURS the Brigadier and the Commanding Officer of 4 Oxford and Bucks reconnoitred in detail the whole frontage of that Battalion including the *Mont des Recollets*. As enemy tanks had been seen north-east of the *Bois de Clairmarais* for several days he also arranged an expedition towards them to try to show offensive tactics. 2 Glos were to send out a section of armoured cars with an anti-tank gun (1 pounder), and a section of 18 pounders with a Royal Artillery Officer to accompany them. They were directed to the place where enemy tanks had been seen to lie up. The party had only travelled a short distance, however, when they came into action against two enemy tanks. After a while the Carrier Section returned and reported that they had lost the anti-tank gun and team, which was believed destroyed.

During the morning a further detachment of Royal Engineers arrived in the town and helped with the process of turning *Cassel* into an impenetrable fortress. More buildings around the town's perimeter were linked by demolition, loop-holed and the walls and ceilings strengthened by props. There was yet more digging where buildings offered no suitable cover. All the roads and lanes were now blocked. Beyond the dense housing, small detachments of the Companies established themselves in more isolated farms and barns that gave good lines of fire down from the hilltop. The officers and men were gratified that they were able to set about these tasks without any attention from the enemy, whose previously relentless drive seemed to abate over the weekend of 25 and 26 May.

It was almost as though the *Panzers* had taken the weekend off. In fact they had been instructed to halt, replenish and regroup while their Infantry caught up with them – the orders coming from Berlin itself. At last it was also possible for the British troops to have some hot meals, some proper sleep and to re-organise the depleted Companies after the losses near *Tournai* and elsewhere. One gruesome reminder, though, of the threat from the enemy was the need to clear up the horrors at the eastern end of the town where the French horse-drawn supply column had been caught in the recent bombing raid. Disposing of the putrefying corpses and body parts (human and horse alike) in the summer heat and with regard to some sort of dignity took a toll on the men, both physically and emotionally.

At 1400 hours a Liaison Officer arrived from GHQ and the Brigadier again pressed for some anti-aircraft guns and at least one Battery of 25 pounders as these would enable him to shell the wood to his front. During the evening a 4-gun anti-aircraft Platoon arrived but there was no sign of any 25 pounders nor crews. GHQ were saving these for other actions although, as it turned out, these guns would have been invaluable at *Cassel* over the next two days. And, ironically, they were

never 'used in anger' after being pulled back to the *Dunkirk* area and
then just abandoned there.

At 1430 hours General Sir *Augustus Thorne*, General Officer
Commanding 48th Division, arrived at Brigade HQ. He reported on the
current overall situation – there was a plan, he said, for a major force
from the BEF to break out from the *Dunkirk* area and push forward
towards the line of the *Gravelines* to *St Omer* canal. It was believed that
the Germans could be forced to withdraw from what was, effectively,
an exposed pocket. He seemed optimistic and made no mention of
any intended withdrawal from *Dunkirk*. He did reveal, though, that the
Allies had been 'badly let down' by the Belgians, who had capitulated. As
far as *Cassel* was concerned, he suggested that some of *Somerset's* troops
should push down beyond the railway line that crossed to the south of
the town to act as outposts and that a Platoon go out to occupy the pillbox about a mile and half north of the town, on the main road up to
Dunkirk.

After the General's departure *Somerset* gave orders to 2 Glos CO
to make preparations for sending a Platoon (under Lieutenant *R.G.
Cresswell*) to the concrete pillbox on the *Dunkirk* road. They were also to
send a Company to *Zuytpeene* (*Gilmore* chose A Company under Major
W.H. Percy-Hardman), two miles to the west of *Cassel*, taking an anti-
tank gun with them. This was to form an outpost in front of the main
2 Glos lines in which position they would be able to disrupt any enemy
approach. He also ordered 4 Oxford and Bucks to send a similar force to
Bavinchove, three miles south west, to perform a similar role.

At about 1530 hours *Somerset* set off on a recce with the
Commanding Officer of the Royal Artillery (RA) leaving his Brigade
Major (second in command) to 'hold the fort'. They first went to
Hondeghem where there were Troops of 18-pounder Royal Artillery and
half a Company of Searchlights, both under the command of a Major
Hoare, RA. *Hondeghem* itself was a small village with flat country all
around it and probably impossible to defend against mobile armour.
Nonetheless the defenders seemed quite happy with their precarious
situation even after *Somerset* told them that they must be prepared for
'all round defence till the last'.

Somerset's party then went to *Hazebrouck* to see the Commanding
Officer of 1 Bucks, the Territorial Battalion he had diverted to the
town 36 hours earlier. It appeared that the previous CO in the town (a
Colonel) had departed as soon as the Bucks Battalion had arrived, and

he had neither handed over formally nor left any information on the heterogeneous collection of troops in the area. The new CO had found elements of almost every unit in the British Army there and members of various ancillary services of all descriptions. In fact, all was chaos and the CO was still trying to organise some sort of defensive structure. This was clearly urgent – the noise of a major fight in and around the *Bois de Nieppe*, just a few miles south, could be heard throughout the town. *Somerset* recorded, in his later account, that 1 Bucks had been faced with a 'tremendous task' as a Territorial unit, especially since there was a ragbag of different elements of the BEF there and that, had there been time, he would have tried to help establish more organisation.

The Brigadier and his companion then travelled north through *St Sylvestre*, *Steenvorde* and *Winnizeele*, villages skirting the east of the *Cassel* massif, to *Wormhout* where a defence was being prepared by Brigadier *Hamilton* of 144 Brigade.

We had tea with Brig Hamilton, and all seemed very peaceful – one could scarcely believe there was a war on.[67]

Somerset and company then returned to *Cassel* along the *Dunkirk* to *Cassel* road. *En route* they inspected the blockhouse, which a detachment of 2 Glos were to occupy that evening. It wasn't very satisfactory as there was, as yet, no steel door, the building was still covered in scaffolding, and the opening was to the south – it having been constructed to resist attack expected from the north and east.

On his return to *Cassel*, Somerset was briefed on his Brigade's first contact with the enemy. Some German tanks and supporting infantry had probed forward from a wooded area below the perimeter held by D Company of 2 Glos. The Germans had been repelled fairly easily and had not reappeared. *Somerset* saw no reason to change his plans and sent off the detachments for *Zuytpeene*, *Bavinchove* and the pillbox. The troops didn't get to these places until just before dark and although it meant that their presence was unknown to the enemy, they had little chance of preparing any forms of defence.

After dark a Lt. Col. of the Royal Engineers passed through the town and called in to Brigade HQ. He had been in *Dunkirk* and told *Somerset* that all non-combatant units were being embarked. This did not seem to support the actuality of a proposed breakout and counterattack and the news left an air of some doubt in the minds of the staff at

Cassel. Nonetheless, the Brigadier sat down with the Commanding Officer of the Royal Artillery units in the town and discussed how best to continue the fight: how best to cope with the enemy tanks that were almost certain to attack the town more aggressively in the very near future. And sure enough, after a few quiet hours of darkness, during which a series of cycle patrols reported nothing beyond the fact that *Dunkirk* itself was again extensively on fire, the enemy put in an appearance at first light.

Monday 27 May 1940

As DAWN BROKE an enemy reconnaissance plane flew low over the town and arrogantly drew a swastika in the sky with dense black smoke. This was evidently a signal to his artillery colleagues for an intense barrage opened up immediately thereafter. Then German bombers came over the town in what was to be only the first of many an unhindered bombardment; the *Luftwaffe* appeared to have complete air supremacy, at least in the *Cassel* area.

2 Glos CO motored out to A Company at *Zuytpeene* to satisfy himself that the depleted Company had been able to dig in there and he found all in order. His departure back up into *Cassel* was delayed by the appearance of a German reconnaissance plane over the village. Back up in the town he found that it was being bombed and mortared once again and he decided not to drive north to the blockhouse.

At 0730 hours, under cover of the bombardment, enemy armed columns moved out from the direction of *St. Omer*, some towards *Cassel* and some towards *Hazebrouck*. Tanks, preceded by motorcyclists and armoured cars, were followed by infantry in armoured half-tracks. The villages of *Zuytpeene*, *Bavinchove* and *Hondeghem* lay directly in the path of the columns. The British soldiers waiting expectantly in their prepared positions along the southern perimeter of *Cassel* had a grandstand view. Suddenly the columns splintered – machines and men scattered: they had come under fire from the three villages. Nonetheless, the enemy forces were vastly superior in firepower and numbers and the Troop of Royal Artillery defending *Hondeghem* was soon overwhelmed: after 1000 hours nothing further was heard from them. And very soon many enemy tanks were reported to be in *St. Sylvestre*. The road between *Cassel* and *Hazebrouck* was therefore completely blocked – from now on *Cassel* and *Hazebrouck* would have to fight separately.

At *Bavinchove* the 4 Oxford and Bucks Company fought desperately to keep back the enemy attack. Situated too far from *Cassel* to hope for any help or reinforcements they fought valiantly for several hours before the remnants managed to extricate themselves and struggle back uphill into the main town.

At *Zuytpeene* the 60-strong contingent of 2 Glos A Company held their positions until about noon but by then they were completely surrounded. A despatch rider sent down from *Cassel*, to be updated on the state of the battle there, was unable to get through. Only five of A Company ever managed to return to *Cassel*. The rest were relentlessly driven back into the heart of the village during a long and dangerous afternoon until the survivors were gathered for a final stand in the cellars of the building they had adopted as the HQ. By 1900 hours the building was a complete inferno and the Germans were throwing grenades down into the cellars. Further resistance was impossible and those who were still able had no option but to surrender.

In *Hazebrouck*, meantime, the ragbag of defending forces was fragmented by the incursion of a large number of tanks into the small town during that morning. But the defenders continued to resist. The minority still standing at dusk withdrew into a redoubt they had prepared in the local convent, but having taken to the cellars the building was then destroyed by *Stuka* dive bombers. The survivors were trapped under masonry with many wounded comrades until the Germans dug them out and forced them to surrender.

For much of the morning there was also a ground attack directed mainly on the south and south-eastern part of *Cassel* itself. Heavy tanks came up under what cover they could get and opened fire with all weapons. They appeared to be trying to get a footing on the saddle of land between *Cassel* and the *Mont de Recollets*. The fire was very accurate and continuous, and the tanks showed great daring. Their crews probably thought that the British soldiers would withdraw as had been happening consistently for the last fortnight. They were to be mistaken and many tanks were knocked out.

The continuous German bombardment – both artillery and mortar – was unerringly accurate. The German reconnaissance plane – which someone had christened 'Our Guardian Angel' – continually spotted Brigade positions so that the German firing was accurately directed, and casualties were high. Many of the British guns were soon out of action. The telephone lines to all the units were constantly cut by enemy fire and this interfered greatly with making arrangements and dispositions. The Signallers repeatedly repaired the lines though under fire and suffered casualties, but for much of the time runners from HQ Company had to be used instead. Brigade HQ and Battalion HQs were repeatedly targeted with unerring accuracy, strengthening the view that there were fifth columnists at work within the town. The Brigadier himself narrowly survived one direct hit:

My staff had gone to lunch . . . while my Brigade Major and I were writing orders. Before we could go to lunch a salvo went straight into the Mess killing the cooks and wounding the staff, including my batman . . . as the fire became fiercer, I was forced to move the HQ to a more sheltered building.[68]

After this both Brigade and 2 Glos HQs were moved to buildings in a smaller town square north of the *'grand place'*, going underground and shielding their entrances with damaged vehicles and sandbags.

After midday the enemy made a very strong push from the south-west and 2 Glos D Company felt the pressure. They began to sustain casualties, particularly when a tank managed to encroach as far as the Company HQ and the anti-tank gun platoon sent to eliminate it was mortared. Captain *Wilson* of B Company, hearing the sounds of a substantial battle, went across the town to see if he could help. He found the floor of D Company's HQ covered in wounded men and a German tank ensconced in the garden of the building. Eventually another anti-tank gun managed to set the intruder on fire. There were also losses for C Company even though they managed to keep the Germans at a distance. Shelling and mortaring of the town continued all afternoon and into the evening. It was difficult to estimate the number of enemy tanks and armoured cars that had been destroyed as different units claimed the same tanks at times. The officer commanding the Anti-Tank Battalion (Major *Ronald Cartland*, younger brother of Barbara Cartland, the novelist, and subsequently killed on 30 May[69]) confirmed at least 25 and others said more.

From 1800 hours there were sounds of an engagement at the blockhouse – the enemy had obviously now encircled to the north of *Cassel*. An armoured car patrol sent out to see if they could help the isolated contingent soon returned to report the presence of many Germans on and around the road down to the blockhouse. The detachment there was obviously now surrounded – as, possibly, was *Cassel* itself.

After the first day's intense fighting in the defence of Cassel there were many dreadful sights to affect those still alive. It was the stretcher-bearers, the medical orderlies and doctors who had to cope with more awful sights and injuries than anyone:

. . . wrapped-up corpses were placed on the back of a truck. It was an unpleasant task but it became routine until one blanket fell open and a severed head rolled onto the ground. Even [the hardened orderly] was shocked by this, but he took a deep breath, picked up the head, placed it back inside the blanket, and sealed it up more securely.[70]

Later in the evening the attacks abated and an uncanny silence was broken only by the cascades of timbers and masonry in all the burning buildings. *Somerset* ordered very active patrolling all round *Cassel* and although on several occasions enemy patrols were reported, no clashes occurred. Fortunately, it rained heavily during the night but although this dampened many of the burning buildings, it increased the misery of the men taking their turn on watch. Crouching in their slit trenches, the blackness in front of them seemed very sinister and the last watch were glad to see the dawn.

Tuesday 28 May 1940

DAYLIGHT REVEALED THAT the enemy had withdrawn from the immediate vicinity of *Cassel* but the garrison had no peace – there was constant bombardment by mortars and artillery. Barricades along the road to *Dunkirk* were now clearly visible and small parties of Germans could be seen running about or digging in all around the town. They were setting light to houses, farms and haystacks, many of which were burning fiercely. A recce to the east reported the enemy in *Steenvoorde* and as they had been in *St. Sylvestre* the day before, 'Somerforce' was obviously nearly surrounded.

The situation all around *Cassel* continued to change as the day progressed. Patrols of light tanks and armoured cars sent out from the town very quickly returned to report the heavy presence of tanks and troops digging in along any direction they cared to probe. The men at the blockhouse were certainly cut off. All the neighbouring villages were now occupied by the enemy. Encirclement was complete: the force was seemingly surrounded. However, the men were resilient after the close quarter fighting of the previous day despite the losses and the fact that the Regimental Aid Post was already full. At long last the Battalions had had the opportunity to stand and fight, to actually use their constructed defences. But the morale of the Brigade took a dent when a Liaison Officer rode into the town to demand that all the 18-pounder guns be given up and transported to the *Dunkirk* perimeter to strengthen the positions there. Higher command, it seemed, were willing to abandon 'Somerforce', leaving them, defenceless, to their fate. *Somerset* compromised and allowed only a few guns and crews to go north and even they, it was reported later, had had to fight their way through and some were damaged.

2 Glos CO toured all his Company positions and found the troops themselves to be still 'in great heart'. As the day progressed however, everyone in the town became increasingly aware of their isolation. From the vantage points the defenders had around the town, enemy movements could clearly be seen in all directions. The wounded with major trauma could not be sent to hospital for proper attention since evacuation was not feasible and there were many deaths that might otherwise have been averted. And to rub in their predicament, food was now running out and everyone was put on short rations.

During the afternoon there was a different kind of aerial bombardment – a plane dropped leaflets over the town. The leaflets were amateurish. They showed a rough plan of the area, that the town was surrounded, and a caption (in English and French) stated *'British soldiers lay down your arms. You are surrounded and your Generals have gone.'* The Brigadier ordered the leaflets to be collected up where possible and destroyed but in the meantime the documents provoked many ribald comments, mostly along the theme that the enemy had been very considerate now that toilet paper was running low.

The Brigadier saw that the orders for the withdrawal of his force must come with no further delay if they were to effect an escape but there was now a breakdown of communications: *Gort* had now moved his HQ further north and all telephonic links were broken. As *Somerset* later recorded,

'I realised we were virtually besieged and that the orders for the withdrawal of my force must surely come at any moment if we were going to be able to make it at all.'[71]

Late that evening a Lieutenant of 4 Oxford and Bucks managed to bring up some rations from *Hondschoote* (on the outskirts of *Dunkirk*) where he had learned some devastating news. He hastened over to *Somerset's* HQ. It was news that *Somerset* had begun to suspect. It was to the effect that the whole BEF was pouring into *Dunkirk* – while the troops at *Cassel* and the other strong-points still strived to hold up the enemy. All other units were parking their transport and guns in fields where they were being systematically put beyond use. There was now no question, as far as one could see, of any counterattack. The BEF was at an end and a mass evacuation was under way. Everyone was embarking as fast as they possibly could.

The garrison (at *Cassel*) had fulfilled its mission but, because no message arrived ordering Brigadier *Somerset* to retreat, he and his men were forced to hold on. In the short term, the principal problem the *Cassel* Battalions faced was not the danger posed by the Germans, who had given the town a wide berth that day, but their own morale. Looking out from their vantage points in the town, they could see that more and more Germans were moving across their line of retreat to the north, as well as appearing in the south. As if that was not demoralising enough, their deteriorating living conditions made life in *Cassel* unpleasant to say the least. Even 145 Brigade's Commander, Brigadier *Somerset*, was somewhat disenchanted on hearing the news from the 4 Oxford and Bucks quartermaster. He later wrote in his account of the campaign:

I now fully realized that we were the 'Joe Soaps' of Dunkirk: that we were being sacrificed so that as many British and French as possible could get away from Dunkirk and get all the kudos for that. I felt very bitter.[72]

However, he quickly pulled himself together (and the quartermaster was sworn to secrecy).* *Somerset* could only hope for the arrival of orders to withdraw – but nothing came that night. There was no real alternative to carrying on the fight into another day. For the night, units were again ordered to carry out active patrolling, but only one enemy squad was encountered and that was early on.

*Nonetheless, Brigadier Somerset was always annoyed, after the war, that the most widely-read historical account of the *Dunkirk* episode in the war (that written by *Winston Churchill*) completely omitted any mention, even, of the courageous efforts of the British Army units that had protected *Gort's* 'escape corridor' and the very heavy sacrifices they made in death, injury or lengthy imprisonment.[73]

Wednesday 29 May 1940

D URING THE NIGHT an enemy plane dropped magnesium flares over the town – perhaps in an attempt to start fires or possibly to illuminate the exact dispositions of the defenders. The latter may be the best explanation for from first light there was sustained and very accurate shelling (heavy mortars and artillery) of certain positions in the town. One shell landed in the kitchen of 2 Glos B Company HQ. One of the Company signallers was blown to pieces and ten others were badly wounded including one man whose legs were blown off. Captain *Wilson* received a small piece of shrapnel in the thigh. Sadly, it took some time before these wounded men could receive proper attention. The stretcher-bearer platoon was heavily engaged elsewhere and moving the men out of the chaos of the room was extremely difficult. It was some time before these wounded men arrived at the Regimental Aid Post. Throughout the morning there was yet more destruction to the fabric of the town and more fresh casualties.

Then, approaching midday, the Germans launched a determined tank and infantry assault on the west and north-west sectors of the town – on the perimeters manned by 2 Glos B and D Companies. The Glosters refused to yield and the attack points spread laterally, the enemy looking for weak spots until the whole town was under attack. The Germans were very persistent but failed to gain a single foothold in the town. About 1430 hours enemy shell and mortar fire grew in intensity and many more casualties were reported. One shell penetrated 4 Oxford and Bucks HQ killing the second-in-command and wounding several officers and other ranks. The Liaison Officer of that Battalion rushed to Brigade HQ with the news and collapsed on arrival. He was covered in the remains of some of his comrades. An outpost detachment of 2 Glos in a farm received a direct hit – the officer was killed and several men wounded. The post was abandoned but was re-occupied later. The enemy were finally driven off during late afternoon.

Meanwhile there had been a major development at Brigade HQ. As *Somerset* recalled later:

At about 1000 hours a Despatch Rider arrived from 48th Division HQ. He was badly shaken and somewhat incoherent having had an encounter with some enemy 'en route'. He should have reached us the night before but said he

had been unable to get through. (Why the orders hadn't come by wireless we
could never discover: we were in touch with Division HQ and sent constant
situation reports). The Despatch Rider had a written order for me. I was to
withdraw my whole force to Hondschoote and to take up a stated position
along the canal there as part of the Dunkirk perimeter.[74]

In view of these orders *Somerset* questioned the despatch rider
on his exact route into *Cassel* since he was probably a good source of
information on the exact whereabouts of the enemy in the immediate
locality. However, the messenger was obviously disorientated; confused,
even, on where he had hidden overnight and was allowed to leave.

Had the orders reached me the previous evening, I think without doubt the
greater part of my force would have got through, but to attempt it in daylight
and in contact with the enemy, who were also astride our lines of withdrawal
seemed out of the question. I therefore radioed to Division that I proposed
withdrawing that night after dark and on the strength of this prepared detailed
orders for the withdrawal.[75]

Somerset did actually receive orders by radio somewhat later in
the day. Division HQ now appreciated that 'Somerforce' was virtually
surrounded and that all transport and guns should be destroyed and
abandoned. The men should move across country to *Hondschoote*
carrying personal weapons only, hopefully without having to engage
the enemy *en route*. *Somerset* decided to amend these orders – he felt
disinclined to abandon his few armoured cars and anti-tank guns since
these might prove useful and he hoped still to be able to move after dark
along the lanes to the northeast – through the villages of *Winnizeele*
and *Watou* – *Hondschoote* would then be directly north, by compass if
necessary. He made an effort to discover the exact situation by sending
out a recce party of one Troop of light tanks and one Troop of anti-tank
guns to proceed along the road to *Winnizeele* and, if possible, on to the
village of *Watou*. If feasible, they were to secure these hamlets and report
back. Hopefully there might just be an escape route for the garrison –
but nothing was ever heard from the recce party after their departure at
1430 hours.

Later in the afternoon, German assaults on the periphery
defences, the mortaring and shelling, all seemed to die down. At the
same time, officers of the Brigade at *Cassel* learned, by word of mouth,

the rumour that the garrison was about to be withdrawn from the town. Sure enough, just after 1700 the Brigade Liaison Officer systematically toured the fighting units inviting each Company to send representatives to a meeting at Brigade HQ at 1945 hours. The whispers were true; orders for an organised withdrawal from the town were to be issued.

At their meeting at Brigade HQ, *Somerset* and his staff faced a very difficult task in planning. At about 1930 hours a wireless message had come in from Divisional HQ but it was in a code that no-one understood. The only orders were still those from GHQ – to retreat – but these had been received some 24 hours late because the Despatch Rider had taken so long to infiltrate through the enemy. The hard fighting of

The 'Grand Place' of Cassel after the battle, May 1940. (Wikipedia commons. Bundesarchiv).

that morning, the losses and casualties, could have been avoided, a very poignant mischance. But almost worse was the fact that the appraisal of enemy positions also brought in by the messenger was now probably so inaccurate as to be dangerous. But, for what they were worth, the situation notes reported that the enemy now occupied *Steenvorde*, the town immediately to the east of *Cassel*. And it had been all too obvious that the Germans were very active immediately north and west of the town – motor vehicle activity had been observed by everyone throughout that afternoon. However, early on the previous day, at least, the road north to *Dunkirk* via *Watou* and *Hondschoote* had still been, reportedly, in Allied hands and it could be that the enemy armoured cars and tanks observed to be on the move all afternoon had not yet been reinforced by infantry. 145 Brigade might just filter through the net around them during darkness. On these rather tenuous hopes, the written orders to each Company were termed in making an ordered withdrawal via *Watou* and *Roesbrugge* (in order to cross the river *Yser*) and thence to *Hondschoote*. *Somerset* was convinced that the enemy would very quickly discover that the Brigade was leaving and would immediately ascend into the town and harass them from the rear. In fact, the Germans didn't react until after dawn and only began moving into the town about 0600 hours the next morning.

After the attack on the blockhouse at 1800 on Monday 27 May, the Platoon there soon found themselves completely surrounded and cut off from *Cassel*. With orders to delay the enemy's approach to the town 'at all costs' they held on heroically. In fact, they held the blockhouse for four days even though their rations ran out and the structure was on fire for much of the time. They tended their wounded as best they could and continued to exasperate the enemy who even brought up tanks. It was only on Thursday 30 May when the silence over *Cassel* indicated that the main force there had left that the platoon tried to break away. However, they were still so closely surrounded that escape was impossible and they were all captured.

8

EVACUATION OF CASSEL AND EVASION ATTEMPTS

Evening of Wednesday 29 May 1940

NAVIGATING A SUCCESSFUL route from *Cassel* was going to be very difficult but some contingent decisions were more straightforward. All transport, excepting armoured cars and Bren gun carriers, was to be put out of action by zero-hour (2130). Vehicles were not to be burned, however, lest this give away the 'show'. All personal kit was to be abandoned and each man was to move with only his weapons and such equipment and rations as could be comfortably carried. 'Phase One' of the strategy was to be a silent, stealthy disengagement from the enemy. It was very fortunate that a relatively quiet evening regards enemy activity and a rainstorm both suggested that this phase, at least, might be achieved. 2 Glos were to steal away from their posts and pass through the men of 4 Oxford and Bucks and on out of the town heading east towards *'Mont des Recollets'*. Other units would follow and then the Oxford and Bucks bring up the rear leaving the town empty. Empty, that is, except for the wounded. There was no possibility of conveying any of the major casualties and *Somerset* was forced to leave them, with one Medical Officer, in the Keep. They numbered about 40. There appears to have been a rather fatalistic attitude among the troops who were leaving:

When it became dusk, we found some piglets and the cooks cooked them. There's always someone who says something wrong: when we were eating in the dark someone said, 'It's the Last Supper'.[76]

2 Glos Companies took up positions on the *'Mont'* from which they would be able to cover the final withdrawal of their colleagues. They

then waited and tagged on to the end of the marching column as a rear-guard as it groped its way forward along the road towards *Steenvorde*. All natural light had now gone and with a dense cloud cover it was a very black night. A small detachment reconnoitred the road ahead for a short distance and reported back that all was clear. The situation was very tense, however, even though all the defence positions in the town had been abandoned without the activity being spotted and without being molested by the enemy. Various buildings in *Cassel* were burning brightly and still highly visible, the road was badly pitted from bomb and shell damage and fallen telephone wires were a great hindrance.

Phase One was now complete but before any real distance had been covered there was an impromptu conference between the Brigadier and some of his officers. Word had now come in of a German anti-tank gun and detachment seen astride the road ahead. If correct it would bar access to the lanes off to the north. Rather than start a firefight and rouse every enemy troop within five miles, *Somerset* conceded that it would be better for the Brigade to go, forthwith, across country following a north-easterly compass direction. It was presumed that this traverse would eventually cross a prospective route – hopefully by road – through *Houtkerque, Oost-Cappel* and *Hondschoote*. There is no comment in the reports but presumably the armoured cars and Bren-gun carriers would have been put out of action at this point and abandoned.

It was perhaps inevitable that this change of plan broke up the structural organisation of the retreat. The fields had, in many cases, deep and very wet vegetation and high, dense hedges. Gates were often in the 'wrong' positions and no-one had any worthwhile maps. Before long there were scares when units suddenly came across each other, sometimes heading in totally different directions. Thankfully no weapons were discharged. 2 Glos managed to stay together but after less than a mile and already having had to negotiate several hedges and wire fences, the Battalion CO, Lt-Col Gilmore, realised that progress was too slow if his men were to reach friendly territory before dawn. He decided that the Battalion would do better to take their chance on the roads and turned them back to resume the route laid out by the initial orders.

Thursday 30 May 1940

ON RESUMING THE ROAD, a platoon of HQ Company was sent forward as advance guard. There was stop/start progress during the remaining hours of darkness but the Battalion reached *Winnizeele* before dawn. Here they found a picket from the East Riding Yeomanry who reported no signs of the enemy. But, having marched a further mile or so, there was suddenly gunfire a short distance ahead of and to the right of the column. This was followed by Verey lights going up and more rapid firing. Silence then resumed. Dawn was just breaking now and with the village of *Droogland* in sight, the silent column suddenly halted and those ahead all lay down. The Adjutant was sent forward to discover the nature of the problem. He returned after 20 minutes to report that a party of 4 Oxford and Bucks had located some Germans in the village and that they were intending to drive them out. 2 Glos resumed their march until reaching a T-junction on the outskirts of the community, Companies being in open order on either side of the road.

There had been no indication of any more action ahead but the column was making tentative progress, on high alert. Suddenly an enemy light reconnaissance plane flew out from the village, very low, along the line of the road, as if searching to see what force was approaching. The CO rapped out an order to lie down and not open fire. In the half-light he hoped that they might not be seen. However, someone at the rear of the column opened up on the plane with a light machine-gun. The plane banked violently, turned, and flew away. The presence of Allied troops was now all too obvious to the pilot even if he had been unable to make any detailed assessment. Within quarter of an hour, with the anxious column still waiting outside *Droogland* village, enemy automatic fire opened up. It was directed straight down the road and coming from several of the houses. Fortunately, it was all too high and there were no casualties. The CO concluded that the village was held in some strength and the exact route north as laid down for the Battalion was therefore blocked by the Germans. He was conscious of the expectation that he should lead his men to *Dunkirk* without engaging the enemy (unless from the rear) and also that his men had only light weapons and little ammunition. It was clear that they should try to infiltrate round the enemy as quickly as possible and regain their route further north. The one remaining map in his possession showed that it might be possible for an encircling movement around the west side of the village where there were lanes and tracks, hopefully with hedges allowing some concealment. It seemed that there might also be some assistance from a mist that was rising.

Headquarters Company and then the other 2 Glos Companies managed to get around the village just as heavy machine-gun and tank fire began to fall on and around the T-junction. There was a very helpful fold in a convenient field and by 0430 hours the Battalion was on the move again as an ordered column led by the CO and preceded by two Privates as scouts. After about a mile they came across a party of Brigade Headquarters under its Colour Sergeant. He informed the CO that the Brigadier and several of his subordinates had either been killed or captured during an engagement in the night.

The column then came across an anti-tank ditch following the line of the Belgian border. It stretched north as far as the eye could see and so the CO led the Battalion into it as it afforded good cover, which the road did not. At a junction with another trench, the CO halted the column to allow it to close up lest one section take the wrong route. Unfortunately, there was poor cover at this point and they were fired at – a single rifle bullet passing overhead of the front of the column. Thankfully this did not presage any other attacks and the column continued as far as the main road running north to *Oost-Cappel*. This was clearly an important highway and best avoided, so the Battalion moved across some gardens and enclosures at the backs of three or four isolated farms and cottages. They were then confronted by a large open space affording no cover. Crossing it, however, would gain them a lane going in the right direction and with high hedges on both sides. The ground mist was still giving a certain amount of cover and a scouting party set off across the open ground. But just as they neared the lane entrance the enemy opened fire and one man was killed. There was then further fire in several short bursts with some of it now towards the head of the column itself. It appeared to be coming down the very lane that had seemed to be the Battalion's most promising route forward. A Bren gun was brought up and responded to the enemy fusillade but to no effect: any further movement towards the lane was met with fierce fire. The enemy then opened up with machine-gun and small shell fire, all seeming to come from the north. C Company was sent forward, under covering fire, to reconnoitre. A significant skirmish developed on the approach to a small hamlet. Meanwhile the CO had traversed to the north-west from where he could see, through binoculars, at least three tanks firing from under cover of some trees 500 yards to the north. With no arms with which to combat tanks and with C Company now taking significant casualties at the hamlet, the CO had to accept that further advance was out of the question. What's more, the morning mist was evaporating and now, at 0800, there was perfect distance vision. C Company pulled back and enemy activity died down. The column had earlier passed a large wood.* It was now about a mile to their rear and the CO gave orders that all companies and detachments were to withdraw separately to this cover. At the same time he sent his one remaining armoured car forward again just to see if there might be another suitable route past the Germans.

Bois St. Acaire 2017.

The Battalion reached the wood about 0900 hours and dispersed within it, grateful for the prospect of shelter and rest especially since there was no more enemy activity. The armoured car now returned and

*   Captain Wilson's published report of the events of this early morning, 30 May 1940,[77] refers to the Companies being ordered to retire to a wood named 'Rue d'Ypres'. However, the report is also appended as follows: *There is a large wood 3 km NNE of Winnizeele called 'Bois St. Acaire' on modern maps. It is the only one of any size in the area and is almost certainly the one described here. In the November 1939 War Diary of HQ 2 Corps held in the Public Record Office (WO 167/148 Pt 1) there is a 1:250,000 scale map enclosed that has 'Rue d'Ypres' inscribed over and to the east of this wood. The inscription probably originally referred to one of the ancient roads running east to Ypres from either Wormhout, through Herzeele and Houtkerque to Poperinge and Ypres or from Cassel through Steenvoorde to Poperinge and Ypres. The map is Sheet 2 of North West Europe, Lille-Ghent Edition GSGS 4042 War Office 1938 and is the one that was probably being used by 2 Glos at the time. It is annotated as being based on earlier French maps and the inscription from one of the French maps could have been misplaced during the compilation of the War Office edition.*

reported to the CO that no route past the Germans appeared possible. The Commander was willing, however, to make a further reconnaissance and set off to do so. Unfortunately, the Germans must have seen the vehicle enter and then leave that part of the wood as they immediately opened fire with mortars, bombarding the remnants of HQ Company. The mortaring became so intense that they were forced to move and found refuge in a trench system just outside the wood. Though initially immune from firing in their concealment, the CO and his small team heard continual mortaring and machine-gun fire – the Germans spent much of the day trying to comb the remnants of the Battalion out of the wood but were unsuccessful. At 1130 hours however, the Germans opened fire on the trench system sheltering Lt-Col *Gilmore* and his party and within minutes enemy infantry with fixed bayonets appeared on the parapet. Resistance was useless. The CO was separated and carried off to *Watou* on a tank, to be interrogated by the nearest senior German officer.

Other detachments, isolated in the wood, fixed bayonets to make a fighting finish as the enemy came closer, but they had no chance as their positions were swept by machine-gun fire. At the corner of the wood, where B and D Companies were trapped, a German called out in excellent English:

Come out! Come out! You are surrounded. Come out with your hands up or we will shell you out.[78]

The remaining men of 2 Glos decided to stay where they were and face the barrage. They remained within the wood and had a nightmare day. Shells and mortars exploding within a forested area create a living hell where red hot metal shrapnel is joined by large shards of splintered wood flying in all directions. Trying to make time pass was an agony – smoking was not allowed lest coughing give away their positions, there was no talking above a whisper and as little movement as possible. The order was given, however, for the men to eat their iron rations.

When darkness finally fell at 2230 hours the men moved off in single file, as silently as possible and keeping to all available cover. After this we only know that scattered parties of men, groups of various sizes, some of them wounded, floundered around in the darkness and were generally captured. A few, however, remained at large for some hours. A dozen men, led by 2nd Lieutenant *Julian Fane*, though suffering a bad shoulder wound, eventually reached *Dunkirk* and were evacuated safely – 12 out of some 700 men of the Battalion that had left England in October 1939.[79]

Another party that tried to sneak away from the wood had rallied around Captain *H C W Wilson*. Although the evidence is only circumstantial, it is very possible that Dad was among the men in this group. He would have known Captain *Wilson* well since this officer had also long served in HQ Company and Dad's recorded date and place of capture fits exactly with the destiny of the group. But whether Dad's precise experience was as one of this group or not, its attempt to reach the Allied perimeter around *Dunkirk* that night is typical of the desperate efforts made to escape detection. Captain *Wilson's* later testimony is both detailed and moving.

About 8 pm we set off. I led with B Company in single file behind me and made the northern edge of the wood where we formed up. At about 2200 hrs, in darkness, we moved off, leaving the wood along the ditch by which we had entered it in the morning. [80]

Once out in the open the men felt very exposed and the enemy were obviously waiting for them, flares at the ready. The party were soon spotted and they came under fire, some of it from machine-guns, and they were mortared. The men scattered in a frantic search for cover, most of them running away to their right, away from the source of the firing. Many fell, however, groaning, or dead. After the hail of bullets and bombs had died away, *Wilson* tried to collect the remainder of his group together in the lee of some earthworks. They recognised the construction as the tank-trap the Allies had prepared during the winter and that ran parallel to the French/Belgian border. When it felt safe to do so the party clambered out of the trench and *Wilson* decided to head further east, by compass bearing, and try to head north later. They froze each time the Germans sent up another flare but made some stop/start progress. They could often hear the enemy shouting to each other.

Nearing midnight the party were spotted by a German patrol and once again flattened themselves as they came under fire in a field of cut hay. Some of the men were hit. Even while the firing continued, the Germans set fire to a haystack to illuminate the area. *Wilson* shouted to his men to run to the edge of the field in the hope that there might be a ditch there. There was, but several of the men remained lying on the field. There was no prospect of going back for the wounded and *Wilson* ordered those unscathed to follow him along the muddy drain until they were swallowed up by darkness. He himself was having increasing difficulty with a stiff and painful leg – he had sustained a shrapnel wound during the defence of *Cassel* – and the ducking and diving of their flight was proving very taxing. The party was also much reduced. It was now down to some fifteen breathless survivors. Their previously bleak prospects were now extremely bleak. Amongst the 'Glosters' there were some stretcher-bearers, and one or two Privates from the East Riding Yeomanry who had somehow attached themselves. Some of the fighting men had lost their rifles and, of course, the Field Ambulance personnel were unarmed. Nevertheless, there was no question that they should not press on.

Friday 31 May 1940

IN A SHORT TIME, the remaining group came to a road running north/ south. Captain *Wilson* signalled a halt and tried to read his map but doing so without showing a light was very troublesome. He had to assume that they had reached the road between *Watou* (to the south) and *Roesbrugge* (to the north). He decided to take his men across the road and then follow it north, keeping about 100 yards distant. The party struggled on through the small hours, climbing fences, pushing through hedges, stumbling over rough ground, and trying not to make any tell-tale noise.

Wilson's report of the next part of the journey does not quite comply with detailed maps of the area, but this is hardly surprising. It was very dark, there was a waning moon and cloud cover. Moreover, *Wilson* only wrote up his account, from memory, some weeks later. But whichever route they had followed, the men came to the bank of a significant river as dawn was breaking. They began to follow it along to their right and some buildings came into view. *Wilson* realised that this had to be the River *Yser* and that the visible community must be *Roesbrugge*. Having ordered a rest-stop, he himself crept forward to make a reconnaissance. He was able to see that the bridge in the village had been blown and took this as a definite indication that the British had abandoned the position to the enemy.

Back with his men, and with daylight getting much stronger, *Wilson* assessed the prospects of their crossing the river and continuing north. Some of the men couldn't swim but a slightly wider and shallower stretch of water had been seen where it was conceivable that they could all wade across. The water came up to their chests, but they managed to reach the north bank and press on across open fields. But after having been 36 hours on the run their luck now gave out. They suddenly came under machine-gun fire.

By rolling and crawling to our right we reached a dip by a fence . . . but a moment later a lorry drew up in a farm lane just behind us. Troops descended from it. Completely surrounded, with our lack of weapons, there was only one thing to do. The men were utterly exhausted from fatigue, lack of sleep and food and seventeen days of continuous fighting or marching. We were prisoners. [81]

At first the newly captured men were frisked, rather violently, for arms and ammunition and began to have their personal possessions stolen. However, the German troops edged back on the arrival of some of their officers. *Wilson* was taken aside and interrogated before they were all marched into *Roesbrugge.* They were taken into a yard where there were already other British prisoners under guard. Although soaking wet, cold and anxious (there had been rumours of summary executions of prisoners by the German Army*) *Wilson* and many of his men fell asleep the moment they were able to sit down. After an hour the prisoners

*The rumours were well-founded. During the invasion of Poland in the previous autumn, some German army units had behaved mercilessly – towards captured troops and civilians alike. There had been many reports of mass executions of prisoners of war, sometimes hundreds at a time.[82] And although the 2 Glos men captured after the fighting at *Cassel* couldn't have known, there had been two recent such atrocities. In the village of *Le Paradis*, about 20 miles south of *Cassel*, about 90 British captives were lined up facing machine-guns in a farmyard soon after surrendering. They realised what was about to happen but there was no escape. Only two survived. It was the afternoon of Monday 27 May.[83] And on the next afternoon, only seven miles from *Cassel* – at *Wormhout*, another of *Gort's* 'strongpoints' – some 70 captured and disarmed men from other Midlands Regiments had been forced, at gunpoint, into a small field barn on the outskirts of the town. The SS troops then threw in hand grenades, ran out of range of the explosions, and proceeded to rake the building with machine-gun fire. No attempt was made to 'finish off' the wounded and only a handful of the men survived their terrible wounds to be retrieved and tended to. They were found to be just alive after a 48-hour living nightmare jammed amongst the blood and bloating corpses of their comrades.[84]

were roused and loaded onto lorries that took them five miles south, to the town of *Watou*. Here there were yet more British prisoners and *Wilson* recognised many of them. As an officer he was separated from his group and taken to a different part of the town where he found other officers including several close comrades from 2 Glos. The Battalion had, effectively, ceased to exist.[85]

9
OFFICIAL STATISTICS FOR THE SECOND BATTALION, GLOUCESTERSHIRE REGIMENT, IN FRANCE 1939/40

THE FIGURES QUOTED IN THE OFFICIAL GLOUCESTERSHIRE REGIMENTAL RECORD FOR THE SECOND BATTALION GLOUCESTERSHIRE REGIMENT IN FRANCE IN 1939/40 ARE AS FOLLOWS: [86]

OFFICERS KILLED 5
OFFICERS TAKEN PRISONER (SOME WOUNDED) 12
OTHER RANKS KILLED 132
OTHER RANKS WOUNDED 57
OTHER RANKS TAKEN PRISONER 472

THE FATES OF the members of the Battalion were officially registered by the authorities on 14 June 1940. It was a record of annihilation – in effect the 2nd Battalion of the Gloucestershire Regiment had been sacrificed and ceased to exist. Nearest relatives were informed shortly afterwards, by telegram. Dad's parents would have been informed that their son was 'missing'.[87] My grandmother always refused to believe that he was dead but it was an anxious 12 weeks before another telegram arrived – on 6 September 1940 – informing them that he was a prisoner of war.[88] And then, sometime in October or November 1940, they would have received his completed 'capture card' informing them of his POW camp, his prisoner of war number and that he was 'in good health'.

On a wall of the Cassel Municipal burial ground, to the south-east of the town, there is a plaque commemorating the participation of the Gloucestershire Regiment in the fighting between 10 May and

29 May 1940.* 19 identified members of the Second Battalion, killed during the actual defence of Cassel, were buried in the graveyard and their named graves are maintained by the War Graves Commission. In addition, there are 20 graves of unidentified British combatants, some of whom would likely have been from the Gloster Battalion. There are also three marked graves of members of the Battalion in the churchyard in the village of Zuytpeene.

The military graveyard at Cassel, managed by the Commonwealth War Graves Commission. 19 members of 2 Battalion, Gloucestershire Regiment are buried here and there is a memorial to the Battalion's action 1940 on the cemetery wall.

* The Fourth Battalion of the Oxfordshire and Buckinghamshire Regiment who had played an equal part in the defence of Cassel suffered equivalent devastation – only four of their men managed to escape to England. They also had colleagues buried in the graveyard at Cassel and share the memorial monument.

10
INTO CAPTIVITY

FOR YOU TOMMY THE WAR IS OVER

CAPTURE BY THE ENEMY, especially in the very midst of a battle, is one of those very critical moments in a life; not, perhaps, comparable to birth but it can certainly lead to premature death. It can be very difficult for soldiers who have been fighting hard, their very lives in jeopardy, to be suddenly responsible for the well-being of captives; those who were, moments before, intent on killing them. But fear of reprisal, of thoughtless or revengeful execution, is only the first of many emotional frames for the new captive.

Putting his arms and ammunition aside and raising his hands in surrender, be it in isolation or in a group, is the beginning of an intense psychological experience for any combatant. Some are just numb, dazed with exhaustion and enclosed in a vortex of death, destruction, body parts, of the screams of the wounded; barely able to grasp their new situation. Others are angry and bitter until their aggression falls away to despair and guilt – 'why am I alive when my friends are dead?' Some captives are disorientated by the profound silence that can follow immediately after fighting. Suddenly becoming acutely aware of wind noise or of birds singing is an unexpected component of so-called 'shock of capture', as is discovering the ability to hold a normal conversation. In fact, a need to share experiences with other surviving comrades can be overwhelming. Battle-hardened officers know that the time at which they are most likely to be able to extract useful information from prisoners is as soon as possible after their captives have surrendered.

If properly treated, if Geneva Conventions are to be respected, prisoners should be quickly escorted to somewhere safe and where the processes of registration and formal captivity can begin. In northern

France in the summer of 1940 the spectacular advances made by the Germans gave them a pretext for making arrangements for the handling of prisoners that were sketchy, if not peremptory and primitive. Most Allied prisoners found themselves herded into open fields ringed by barbed wire – 'cages' – and supervised by trigger-happy guards. There was usually no shelter, virtually

*'For you, Tommy, the war is over'.
(Wikimedia Commons. Bundesarchiv).*

no food or drink and nowhere for bodily functions to be performed. But despite all the horrors and the profound uncertainty of their future, most men started their captivity by simply going to sleep. They were lucky if they were not beaten or robbed.

The prisoner of war (POW) cages soon filled beyond their capacity even though there was rapid turnover. Men were bludgeoned into random groups and then into columns and handed over to reserve German troops. These were not of high calibre and could be cynical and cruel – the *Frontkameradenschaft* – 'front line gallantry' – soon evaporated. Personal looting was widespread. On the pretence of searching for hidden arms, the replacement guards robbed the prisoners of their wallets, watches, rings, pens, money, family photographs and, especially, any cigarettes. Most Allied POWs found that all they had left were the clothes they were wearing (very few in many instances) and these were usually ragged and dirty already from the many days of hard fighting. There was consolation for some if they had been lucky enough to stay among friends. The newly isolated would be seen wandering among the other prisoners in the (often vain) hope of finding a face they might recognise. Their instinct to make bonds was highly appropriate – remaining a stranger and alone, of having no close and trustworthy 'mucker', would become a particular hazard in what was to follow.

The transfer of Allied captives from the battlefields of northern France and Belgium is an aspect of POW experience that has been overlooked and most people are unaware of how horrific it was. It was one of the most taxing times for most of these POWs. The Germans had established (or were still doing so in many instances) permanent POW camps (*Stammlager – Stalags*) well within the boundaries of the Reich.

By policy, many were in conquered areas of Poland, many hundreds of miles from Flanders and a particularly daunting distance from home for British prisoners.

THE MARCH INTO GERMANY

B Y DAWN ON Tuesday 4 June 1940, as the few remaining fortunate groups of defeated BEF troops were taken off the beaches east of Dunkirk and transported back to southern England, some 40,000 British soldiers found themselves left behind.

Those left in France were exhausted beyond belief, racked by hunger, pitifully dishevelled, scared, bewildered and bitter. Moreover, they were about to face up to life as slaves to Hitler's dark dream of European domination.[89]

Most of this unfortunate remnant, about one in six of the BEF, were, if still alive, captive. Most of these POWs, many of them lightly wounded or concussed, were already on the move across northern France and Belgium. Alongside French, Belgian and Dutch prisoners they found themselves formed into large columns and, under constant threat of being shot, force-marched along secondary roads and tracks. The route was often tortuous but the general direction was eastward – towards the German border. Any transport still functioning in the wartorn region was given over to replenishing the German military. However, captured officers – quickly separated from their men after surrendering – were sent to officer prison camps in Germany – *Offizierlager* – 'Oflags' – via the few trains that were still running across Flanders. They might have complained less about their slow and interrupted journeys by 3rd class carriage if they had known how their men were suffering. The Germans assumed that 'other ranks' would create fewer problems if unled. And they were seen as very unlikely to try to escape if weak from thirst, starvation and ceaseless marching. The German expediency arose from wanting to sideline the minimum number of troops from frontline activities that was consistent with prisoner safekeeping, whatever the inhuman consequences.

The Germans set to guarding POWs were mostly second-rate troops who sensed their inadequacies and were often bitter older men who felt that, having survived the First World War, they had already 'done their bit'. Some of the veterans, indeed, seemed hell-bent on revenge for the humiliation of their defeat in the autumn of 1918. Their resentment and insecurity might be understandable but they were most certainly brutal and often sadistic. If they had been made aware of the provisions of the Geneva Conventions for POWs they seemed to choose to ignore them. Few hesitated before shooting men who were at their mercy and totally unarmed. This may have been a systemic feature of the *Nazi* war machine but even within international guidelines the men guarding Allied prisoners on their journeys across northern France were callous at best, at times barbaric. Their officers were completely out of order in not allowing any registration of their charges. The prisoners were, at this stage and, indeed, until they eventually arrived at POW camps, an anonymous mass of disposable humanity. No-one would know nor could know of their fate if they were killed or collapsed or died of wounds. The columns were pushed along at gunpoint anything from 15 to 30 miles a day.

The Geneva Conventions stated the maximum distance for any march should be twelve miles (twenty kilometres). As one soldier recalled, whenever he asked the guards how much further they had to go the answer was always the same – 'three kilometres'. That became the terrible reality for the marchers – it always seemed that rest was somewhere in the distance, just over the next hill, in the next village, another mile, another hour, another day.[90]

Most of June that year was blazing hot and the men had no protection from the sun. They were given virtually no food nor even water, and overnight stops were mostly spent lying on the ground whatever its condition.

Overnight stops were made in all manner of locations, a waterlogged field, a dung-covered farmyard, a dry weed-infested moat, a sports stadium, depending on circumstances. In the main the prisoners had to make do with sleeping outdoors, curled up on bare earth, hoping and praying that it wouldn't rain during the night.[91]

Thirst was overwhelming and nicotine withdrawal for smokers came a close second. Local women, taking pity on the suffering they saw passing through their communities, put out buckets of water for the prisoners to drink. The men eyed them desperately only to watch the guards kick them over. Many of the prisoners became so desperate that they risked darting out of the column and gulping dirty water from animal troughs or ditches. Likewise, they ran into fields or garden plots of growing vegetables, pulled up whatever they could find and ate their trophies raw. Some were shot in their frantic attempts to assuage their needs. Others had no strength beyond staggering onward supported by friends. And there are too many independent reports to doubt the fact that some of the men who collapsed and just couldn't continue were summarily shot in full view of their companions, their bodies dumped at the side of the road. Some who fell and were unable to get up were perhaps more fortunate. They might be dragged to a lorry at the back of the column and lifted aboard but few were ever seen again. There were others who, without real provocation, were attacked by the guards and such assaults could be lethal.

'One incident sickened me', a Sergeant recalled, 'a young boy ahead of me bent down to lace his boot. Instantly a German was on him, and thrust the bayonet up his arse and out his side. He was stretched out on the road as we went by; the agony on his face haunts me still.'[92]

Most men, even after suffering the horrors of battle, were unable ever to forget inexcusable incidents such as this and were affected all their subsequent lives: such unwarranted cruelty was the seed-corn of lifelong flashbacks and nightmares.

Even the fittest, strongest men in the columns had their will to survive severely tested. All became infested with lice and many were struck down with disease. It is no surprise that after scrabbling in dustbins for food scraps, chewing soiled grass and roadside weeds, or consuming the little food they were given out of dirty containers or even their helmets, colicky abdominal pains and diarrhoea became commonplace. Prevented from attending, properly, to the needs of nature and with no ability to clean themselves in any case, the few clothes that most of the men were wearing were soon horribly caked with faeces and the columns began to stink. Eyes were discharging, mouths were dry, tongues raw, lips were split, skin was sunburnt and body flexures were rubbed raw by the rough battledress khaki. The men began to appear barely human. Bent, bearded and filthy, the list of miseries they had to endure could hardly have been longer. The guards even protracted their suffering for political reasons.

Some groups found themselves marching in circles. Suddenly, after miles of marching, they found themselves back in a village they had already passed through. It soon appeared this was a deliberate policy. They were being paraded through as many villages as possible to . . . reinforce the notion that the Allies had been hopelessly crushed.[93]

As exhausting day succeeded exhausting day the prisoners began to crave for nothing more than rest. They soon realised the advantage of being at the front of the column for when stops were allowed those first to arrive at the location got most time off their feet. Those trudging along at the rear often only arrived at the rest place as the head of the column was being kicked to get up and get started. In fact, the prisoners began to develop a primeval instinct towards survival that was entirely self-centred. Anything not secured was prone to theft. All notions of 'fair play' disappeared – men learned that to grab at what was available and never mind his neighbour in the queue was the only real way to get through. Most successful were the close partnerships that grew up – one man to guard belongings while the other went hunting for anything that resembled food, or drink, an abandoned groundsheet, an intact boot, a piece of cloth, a mess tin – anything that might come in useful.

As those who didn't give up dragged themselves, often supporting wounded colleagues, across the border into Germany they were heartened by the rumour that the remainder of their journeys would be by train. This was not to be the good news that they welcomed.

DEEPER INTO THE BAG

FOR THE DESPERATE men forced to trudge across something like 250 miles of France and Belgium there was respite of a sort when they finally reached German territory: the marching stopped. But their distress otherwise was unremitting. Most were shepherded to a transit camp – a *'dulag'* (*Durchgangslager*) – on the outskirts of *Trier*, sometimes only after being paraded around the town through taunting and abusive citizens.[94] The camp was just open land surrounded by barbed wire and machine-gun-toting guards. There was no shelter from the elements and there was huge overcrowding. There was some food once a day but it was only watery soup resembling used washing-up water at best and only for those who still had some sort of receptacle available. The ground conditions within the compound were execrable. The prisoners had no choice but to defecate anywhere and the scraps of paper many had used to try to clean themselves were blowing around like diabolic confetti.

The stench of dirty bodies and human ordure was all-pervasive as was the emotional despondency. Now not having to rally every last ounce of energy into forcing their aching bodies onward the men began to have thoughts of home and of their predicament. Anxieties crowded in. How could they let their families know that they were still alive, what had happened, what condition they were in, what next? They also had to cope with the prevalent rumours – that Britain was about to be invaded and that its ports and inland cities were already being bombed. Married men, especially, suffered terrible worries and the agonies of knowing there was nothing they could do to help or console their wives and children.[95]

After hours or days at *Trier* and other *'dulags'* it was almost good to be on the move again but there was yet more malice and brutality waiting for them at the railheads. The prisoners found themselves bunched up alongside rows of cattle-trucks that were shunted into sidings. More and more men arrived and there was squirming and pushing to get to the front as fears of being left behind reached a crescendo. As the loading process began this particular anxiety soon receded.

The guards were in a hurry to get the job done . . . they started rounding up groups, pushing them at gunpoint towards the doors like livestock going to market, perhaps to be slaughtered . . . we were helpless to do anything except wait our turn.[96]

The guards were obviously under orders to cram as many prisoners as was (in)humanly possible into each wagon. And they were in no mood to risk the displeasure of their officers. Some of the transports were labelled 'for 40 men or 8 horses' which, even under the painful circumstances, provoked a few wry smiles and raised eyebrows. Men were pushed and kicked, bludgeoned with rifle butts and forced together into each cattle-truck until it was so full that there was, literally, standing room only.

The Germans made no attempt to count how many were going into each wagon. Men who had slumped down on the floor found themselves trampled on as the space got increasingly crowded and the doors were slammed shut . . .[97]

When the guards were satisfied that it was impossible to load any more men into each truck the doors were slid across and the human cargo locked in. With the doors bolted behind them the men found themselves in darkness and it soon became unbearably hot. The only light and air were through narrow horizontal slits just below the roof. It took only minutes for the prisoners to realise their awful predicament.

Inside was as bad as you imagined. There was dirty straw on the floor and a dreadful smell of excrement and urine left behind by recently transported livestock or another human cargo. Before the doors were shut some pails of water were put in and someone threw in some loaves of bread (which turned out to be stale when they were shared out) and a couple of round cheeses.[98]

The prisoners were packed in so tightly, generally 60 or more per wagon, that it was only possible to sit down in turn, and then only with knees pulled up under the chin. Lying down was out of the question. Some trucks carried wounded men and in some lucky cases a blanket was available to make a hammock for them. They were suspended high up in the truck. This

German soldiers loading cattle trucks – here Russian Prisoners of War – (Wikimedia Commons. Bundesarchiv).

was where some of them died (and where their corpses continued to swing gently with the rocking motion of the train until journey's end).

It took only minutes for a dismal silence to descend. The men stood like unsteady skittles or, if lucky, sat huddled in their misery. Even if they all agreed to use one corner of the truck as a latrine it was often impossible to get there before their loose bowels delivered. The odd bucket or helmet given over to use as a receptacle might be passed round but trying to empty it through the high side opening of the truck could be disastrous: the foul contents could blow back in the slipstream. In any case, as their nightmare journeys proceeded, many men found their limbs numb and unresponsive after being pinioned for hours in awkward positions and were forced to release their waste into their clothing or just where they were trapped. And only occasionally did anyone possess, any longer, anything strong and sharp enough to gouge a hole in the floor of the truck to let waste drain away. Conditions under foot were soon worse than many a neglected farmyard. Thirst and hunger returned even in the face of the nauseating stench. Men were prone to retching and the craving for nicotine was far from helpful in smokers (as most were).

Their journeys weren't even direct and uninterrupted. Wherever it was they were heading – the men somehow sensed that it was generally eastward and deeper into the *Reich* – they were making very slow progress. The trains seemed to stop and wait for hours in sidings, often in scorching sunshine, while other trains overtook them. Only once a day, if that, was there a scheduled stop in some remote location when the doors were slid open and the prisoners allowed down onto the lines to stretch their limbs and take some air. Malicious guards and incapacitating faintness precluded any thoughts of escape. Sometimes some soup and bread were made available at these stops but now virtually no-one had any clean containers. The bread might have been welcome but with the consistency (and probably constituted partly) of compacted sawdust it did little for hunger and heightened thirst. Clambering back up into their trucks with more and more reluctance and with more and more difficulty, the prisoners wondered how many more hours, how many more days, they could survive.

Even the oblivion of sleep became impossible. At best the men managed to cat-nap but even these periods of true rest were frequently broken by a swaying neighbour bumping into them or by someone desperately trying to push through the huddle. In fact, many men were afraid to sleep:

The feeling of suffocation was immense, what with being locked inside this hellish crate, pressed up against other men's stinking bodies, you could imagine yourself just drifting into unconsciousness and never waking up again.[99]

These nightmare journeys continued for, on average, three or four days and nights until arrival at far-flung destinations in eastern Europe, places with exotic names in an unfamiliar language and with horizons that could be anywhere short of Siberia. The men disembarked with great difficulty. Some didn't.

I had difficulty getting out, crawling along the truck floor after the others to get to the door. My knees and legs nearly buckled under me as I touched the ground with my feet . . . then you saw where you had ended up after all that travelling – another dirty railway station siding in some scrubby countryside in the middle of a country you'd never heard of . . . [100]

ARRIVAL AT STALAG VIIIB, LAMSDORF, SILESIA

THE MEN HOWLED at and harried out of the stinking cattle-trucks that arrived in sidings next to *Lamsdorf* station in Silesia in early June 1940 blinked at a dreary, flat landscape covered in pine forest. Not that they were intent on their surroundings. They were struggling to stand,

Lambinowice (Lamsdorf) railway station where POWs were assembled before being marched off to Stalag VIIIB.

to summon enough energy to march away from the station, as they were soon ordered to do by impatient armed guards, some manning machine-guns.[101] They staggered along a path through the pines for about a mile and then left onto a road that passed a vast, ominous and densely packed graveyard – the burial place of thousands of POWs from the last conflict, Russians and other Slavs that had succumbed to a typhus epidemic in 1917. Then to the right, along a paved forest track past some substantial brick buildings (guard accommodation) until the path opened onto a huge clearing, and there it was – *Stammlager* (main camp) – *Stalag VIIIB*.

The camp was vast. It was reckoned to be a square with each side about half a mile long. Surrounded by tall,

Stalag VIIIB 'Lamsdorf'. (Wikimedia Commons).

double-banked fences topped with barbed wire and with guard towers spaced at intervals, there were eight separate compounds within. Each contained rows of four single-storey brick-built huts painted white and there were internal roadways running between them.[102] When the men eventually entered one of these huts they found double rows of wooden bunks and a central ablution area in the middle. The floors were of concrete and there was, usually, a stove for heating in winter at each end of the hut. Each hut could house as many as 200 men.[103] But new arrivals would not be aware of their new surroundings until they had been processed.

Lamsdorf was the name the invading Germans had imposed on the small Polish town of *Lambinowice*, about a mile from the camp itself. The town is about 30 miles southwest of *Opole*, the nearest significant community and midway between the cities of *Wroclaw* and *Katowice* in *Silesia*. *Lambinowice* is in a rural situation just to the west of an extensive and densely populated industrial area powered by the many coal mines in the area. And although the border with Czechoslovakia was only 35 miles to the southwest this was now purely a technicality: all of this part of Europe was now part of the 'Reich' and totally under German domination.

There had long been a prisoner of war camp at *Lambinowice*. It was originally established to house French prisoners during the Franco-Prussian war – *Silesia* had also been German in the 1870s. The camp was refilled during the First World War, some of the prisoners being

British, and then again – for Polish POWs – during the autumn of 1939. These men were then to be completely outnumbered by the huge influx of Allied prisoners (mainly British) arriving from June 1940. In fact, the camp was known, locally, as *Britenlager* and eventually every third Briton in uniform who was captured by the Germans found himself at *Stalag VIIIB*.[104] Overcrowding became such a problem by 1943, despite most prisoners being out on work parties, that a subsidiary camp was built some 100 miles to the south at *Český Těšín* (*Teschen* in German) on the original Polish/Czechoslovakian border and the split complex was renamed *Stalag 344*.

On arrival at the camp the bedraggled and exhausted column was broken up into groups of about 50 men and each party taken, in turn, into a wide enclosure at the front of the camp – the *Vorlager*. Guards sitting at trestle tables recorded the details of each prisoner – full name, rank, army number, regiment and company, date of birth, place of birth, father's name and address, mother's family name, civilian occupation prior to enlistment and religion. Date and place of capture was also recorded. Each man was then issued with an identity tag, to be worn around the neck, which was stamped with his name and a unique five-digit POW number.[105] Although rectangular in shape, the men always referred to the

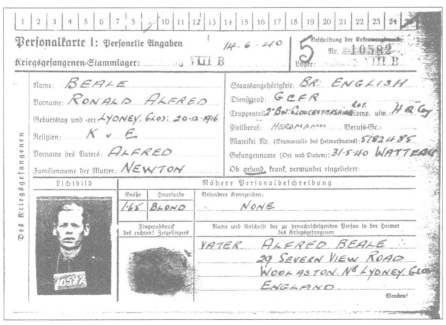

The German prisoner of war registration card for 5182485 Lance Corporal Beale, Lamsdorf 14 June 1940.

tag as their 'disc'. They were each photographed wearing a label showing their POW number, and finger-printed (right index finger). Height and hair colour completed the registration details. However perfunctory and impersonal the reception, the men recognised, with relief, that they had at last been recorded as having a continued existence. Many of the captives had begun to fear that they had already been given up for dead by wives or mothers and if consigned to an anonymity, as they had been until now, what was to stop the Germans killing them anyway? They also hoped that this registration process would lead to their relatives at home being informed of their survival and location but no-one would answer such questions.

It was also strangely reassuring that they were put through a de-lousing process – why would the Germans bother if they were just going to be exterminated? Stripped of their filthy clothing (which was then thrown into large vats of boiling water) the naked men were forced into showers where they found the water to be oscillating wildly between scalding hot and freezing cold. The soap provided seemed to be a suspension of fine grit in a wax and was virtually useless. They then joined a cursing scuffle all trying to identify their own, still damp, uniforms and underwear. They were then, finally, allowed through the main gates of the camp and British NCOs helped them to find empty bunks in the huts. At last they had some personal space and the ability to lie down and rest. They were spending their first few hours as *Kriegsgefangene* – war prisoners, a term that was soon Anglified to 'Kriegies'. After joining in one or two of the ill-tempered scrambles that signified the serving up of food, the new prisoners began to explore their surroundings. Most new arrivals at *Stalag VIIIB* assumed that they were somewhere in Germany – perhaps near Berlin or Munich, cities they knew of. They were surprised to find themselves in what had been, formerly, Poland. The huge distance from home was, of itself, dispiriting and the only distant horizon was to the south – the *Eulengebirge* (owl hills) that were near the frontier with former Czechoslovakia.

YEAR ONE OF CAPTIVITY

STALAG LIFE

S EASONED TROOPS IN any army, and especially hardened 'regulars', expect to find a stringent routine in military life, and days in POW camps proved to be no exception. After a night's rest (of a sort) in a three-tiered wooden bunk softened only by a thin palliasse (mattress bag) under-filled with straw and beneath two coarse blankets, the *kriegies* were roused and released from their huts in time for 8 am *appel* – roll call. They were forced to stand outside in ranks, whatever the weather, until a head count had been performed (often more than once) and announcements made. There was no breakfast, merely the issue of *ersatz* coffee (burnt barley in water, no milk or sugar). Mornings dragged. In 1940 there were no books, no playing cards, no writing materials, no organised activities and no satisfying way of killing time.[106] There was an air of degradation. There was an all-pervading malodour arising from rotting potatoes, at best, or the open cess pits at worst. If it wasn't raining the men shuffled about the camp in their derelict uniforms and, if their boots had finally collapsed, the clogs given out as replacements. Then the new arrivals discovered that the de-lousing process their clothes had undergone had failed. Enough body louse eggs had survived the hot water dousing that a new generation of lice began to plague the men, the ceaseless itching adding to their misery. Inevitably the highlight of every day in camp was the midday issue of food – or what was presented as food. It was always the same. The main meal was watery soup with bread or potatoes. The canny customer hung back from the front of the queue despite his hunger in the hope that he might receive something, anything, solid from the depths of the concoction. This might be a semi-solid piece of vegetable, a fragment of bone with some flesh still attached or even, rarely, an actual piece of meat.[107] And the men soon learned to eat the potatoes without skinning them lest they reveal the rot within.[108] Bread and 'grease' (a fatty spread of dubious origins) was always the fare at 5 pm – at so-called supper. A coarse dark brown loaf would be issued, one to every five men. The POWs soon learned that the width of their 'discs' coincidentally marked out just about a fifth of a standard loaf and after slicing the men drew lots for first and subsequent choices to see fair play. And that was it for the day. It was extremely poor nutrition even for men who were not used to refined foods and who were obliged to be physically inactive. It was a diet totally lacking in a host of essential minerals and vitamins and didn't even stay the men's chronic hunger.

It was no surprise that morale about the camp soon plummeted to very low levels. So low that when the men learned that, NCOs apart, they were going to be sent out, compulsorily, on work parties – Arbeitskommando – as slaves for the Reich, they were almost pleased.[109] They allowed themselves to be persuaded that their food and accommodation would be better, they would not be so confined and that they were even going to be paid. The promises were unfulfilled in most cases and the money turned out to be Lagergeld that could only be spent at certain outlets where there was, they found, virtually nothing to buy. The men soon found other uses for the worthless notes including lighting their cigarettes and cleaning their bottoms.

Kriegies had no privacy. There were up to 200 men in each hut and they were locked in after 'supper'. Toilet facilities overnight consisted of a bucket or two in each hut. Not that the lavatories available during the day were much better. Men relieved themselves sitting at long benches with holes in that were propped above pits.[110] The accumulated excrement was carted away from time to time but the offensive smell, the clear evidence of vermin and the total lack of privacy made attending to bodily functions repulsive.

ARBEITSKOMMANDO

THERE IS A SANITISED view of the experiences of Allied POWs in World War 2 that is both prevalent and persistent. It stems from the flood of books, films and TV series that were produced in the decades immediately after the war ended. They virtually all centred on camps for officers only (Offizierslager) such as the familiar adapted castle on the outskirts of the northern German town of Colditz. British officers – confined separately from their men – did not have a pleasant time as prisoners and, having carried greater responsibilities than the men they led, many harboured a more intense guilt for their defeat. Their desires to continue 'smashing the *Hun*' and to exercise their professional military skills were now almost completely frustrated. Indeed, they were totally denied to them if one discounts the very few who managed to escape or who devised significant sabotage. They lost the prospect of battle honours and of accelerated promotion that is usual in war. But they were able, in large part, to control their own daily routines and activities.[111] For British and Commonwealth POWs, the Germans followed the Geneva Conventions that officers were not obliged to work. Therefore, these middle-class, literate and generally assertive men were able to adapt themselves to use their time in study, with music, amateur entertainments and other communal activities that included organised preparations towards escape. They were able to learn new skills and acquire more qualifications. Their camps – generally on a smaller scale and more sanitary – have been described as a mixture of 'severe boarding school and strict holiday camp' and most of the officer class were already used to the former.[112] This was the stereotype (think Jack Hawkins or Kenneth More) that continues to obscure the much more taxing and purposeless lives of captive 'other ranks'. It is entirely justified that these less privileged '*kriegies*' have been called 'Hitler's slaves' for, unlike their officers, they were forced to work for the *Reich* in factories, mines, quarries, forests and farms under heavy and, at times, brutal oppression.

Within a few days of arriving at *Lamsdorf*, a camp for 'other ranks', the very earliest arrivals were being sectioned off to *Arbeitskommando* – work parties. With a *schadenfreude* that was far from subtle, the Germans seemed to allocate work to each man that was the opposite to his previous experience.[113] Farm labourers were sent to mines or factories, factory hands and mechanics were allotted to agricultural work, office workers condemned to break rocks in quarries. Even the new prisoner who claimed that he had been a lion tamer evoked no particular reaction. Office routines may be tedious but require little physical strength. Mining is hard, dangerous work but those working deep in the earth develop a muscular physique if they can avoid injury. The majority of the men now had to make enormous adaptations that sometimes proved impossible. Moreover, by the time the first work parties were marched out of *Stalag VIIIB*, all the men were weakened and wasted whatever their former prowess. And some were already ill.

They had been sapped by hard fighting, by the traumas of capture, by forced marches, by starvation, by gruelling rail journeys and already by the poor diet and congestion they had found in the camp.

The German record card of the work parties ('Arbeitskommando') on which 5182485 Lance Corporal Beale was sent during his imprisonment.

Dad's experiences were typical in these regards. Captured at or near *Watou* on the French/Belgian border on Friday 31 May 1940, his induction at *Stalag VIIIB* was on Friday 14 June. His registration form was one of those retrieved by British Military Intelligence (probably via the Russians who overran the camp in the spring of 1945) and is shown on page 89. Another element relating to his imprisonment is his work card (in German) (see above).

Dad had only been in *Stalag VIIIB* for a few days when he was sent out on his first work party. On Saturday 22 June he was among a detachment of POWs that travelled to a *Siemens* factory at *Labedy*, a village on the outskirts of the city of *Gliwice*, 60 miles to the east of *Lamsdorf*.[114] He worked in the production plant at *Labedy* for six months, living, with his fellow prisoners, in some sort of camp or compound near the factory. *Siemens*, one of the largest industrial enterprises in pre-war Germany, produced, mainly, electrical components and machine parts but the output was very diverse. Its importance obviously increased when German industry became geared towards war. The company management was deeply infiltrated by the SS and there were soon no scruples in employing (and abusing) a workforce taken from POW camps and concentration camps alike. The exact mix of the work they undertook is unknown but it would almost certainly have been mind-numbing and tedious and for long hours, probably six days a week. The men would have been wearing the clothes in which they had been captured or a variety of second-hand garments they had come across (mostly discarded uniforms of other armies, some of them bloodstained) and they were lucky if they were not lousy. Whether the food was better and more generous, as the Germans had promised, is doubtful. Dad worked in the factory for six months but at least two gratifying things happened during this time.

'Arbeitskommando' – POWs from Stalag VIIIB working in a quarry. (Wikimedia Commons. IWM.)

WRITING HOME

A T AN UNCERTAIN time after arrival at POW camp the prisoners were presented with a means of contacting home. Many new prisoners had assumed that there was, somehow, some hidden bureaucratic machinery that had been set in motion to get news of their capture to relatives back in the UK but this was a false premise.

Knowing that his family would have received news that he was missing and were unaware of his survival, many newly captured prisoners suffered great mental anguish . . .[115]

There was really only one mechanism for making contact with home, for giving them news and for setting up possible return correspondence. This comprised the 'capture card', an impersonal postcard that could only be completed in a most peremptory way but, assuming it got through to the UK (many didn't), at least brought huge relief to thousands of relatives that their serving man was no longer 'missing' (dead by implication).

Thank the Lord you are safe, my darling, wrote Lance-Corporal C's wife to him, *I never want to go through another three months like I have done again.*[116]

The capture cards, a requisite of the Geneva Conventions, were supposed to be made available to POWs within a week of their arrival at a permanent camp but this ruling was often ignored. Thereafter each POW was supposed to be supplied with four postcards and two letter forms each month thereafter; another rule that was often 'overlooked' by the German authorities. But however tenuous the beginnings, two-way communications with home were a vital boost to morale both for the POWs and for their families. In fact, knowing that their relatives at home were safe despite the stories of widespread air raids was a huge comfort for the prisoners. It was not that unusual for men to have survived the horrors of battle and the rigours of being taken into captivity to then find that their nearest and dearest at home had been bombed out of their homes or even, at worst, been injured or killed in the *Blitz*.

SAVED BY THE RED CROSS

THE OTHER CRITICAL development that occurred was later during the autumn of 1940 (just in time for Christmas for many prisoners). It was soon very clear to the POWs newly arrived in their camps across the Greater Germany that, unless there were to be improvements, the food provided for them was inadequate. By instinct alone, never mind their chronic hunger, the men could sense that the obvious deficiencies in both quality and quantity of their rations were going to lead to weakness, weight loss, illness and eventual death by starvation. Article 11 of the Geneva Conventions demanded that POW food provision was to be equivalent to that supplied to their guards. This was blatantly and systematically ignored: the frighteningly small amount of food given to the POWs was not from a temporary logistical blip following the unexpected capture of so many Allied servicemen. There was no prospect of improvement when the POWs were being malnourished by policy.[117]

By the middle of autumn 1940 the men captured earlier that year in France were thin and weak and a growing number of them were sick. They were saved by the International Red Cross scheme in which food parcels (millions of them by the end of the war) were prepared in Britain and Canada (and later also in America) and a protected shipping route opened up through Portugal, the south of France and Switzerland.[118] The men regarded the food parcels (correctly) as lifesaving and although there were predictable problems in their final distribution, especially to the men out on work parties, the bulk of them got through at the expected rate – about one per man per fortnight. There was a double boost to morale – the men were cheered hugely by the familiar trade names – *Typhoo, Oxo, Cadbury, Campbell, Peak Frean*, and *Players* cigarettes. And, before long, the prisoners realised that many of the contents of their parcels were food items that were no longer available anywhere in Germany and could therefore be used to bribe selected guards in return for small favours that further eased the burdens of their imprisonment.[119]

When I came to open my parcel I was overwhelmed to the point of tears – like all the others – and we were a tough bunch of men by now. There were tins of meat, fish, butter, condensed milk and so much else. There was a quarter of a pound of chocolate. There was cocoa. Above all, transcending almost any of the items other than the cigarettes, there was a two-ounce packet of tea.[120]

Red Cross Parcel – one of nine million life-saving packages sent to Allied POWs during the war. (Wikimedia Commons. National Museum American History).

NEVER-ENDING WORK

D AD WORKED AT *Labedy* until the end of 1940 before being transferred to another work party – E88.[121] On Thursday 19 December he was taken a further 20 miles east through the bleak Silesian winter countryside to *Ligota*, a village in the administrative domain of the city of *Chorzów (Königshütte)*, though it was nearer to *Katowice*. Here he found that he was to work down a coal mine – *Königshütte Ostfeld*. Mining was the destiny most feared among the men but there was no avoiding it if you were chosen. Even ex-miners tried to avoid this work if they could.

But a slave has to do his master's bidding and working down a pit was a common destiny for many men from *Stalag VIIIB*. Another POW from *Stalag VIIIB* has described his first hours and days at another mine in the same coalfield. *Ostfeld* was a typical deep mine of the Silesian coalfield and was manned, mostly, by local Polish miners who were experienced in the work and aware of the hazards. They were made responsible for teaching the new (foreign) recruits how to work safely although there were major problems related to language difficulties. The typical experience of prisoners such as Dad was written up after the war and is a precious first-hand testimony:

Once again we embarked on cattle-trucks for a twenty-four-hour journey from Stalag VIIIB to our new destination . . . our new quarters were within the confines of the coal mine grounds but separated from the mining complex by a barbed wire fence . . . the camp was made up of a row of terraced huts, each self-contained with its own door and accommodation for eight men . . . in front of the huts was an open space approximately 20 yards wide and 60 yards long. This was used for daily roll call and for queuing for food issue morning and evening.[122]

Men finding such conditions were encouraged at first – the accommodation was certainly better than back at *Stalag* – but this was small compensation for the conditions they would find underground.

Our introduction to the coal mine came on the third day at 6.30 am. The majority of the miners were Poles but the overseers were German. Each prisoner was assigned to a particular Pole and we were to remain with him for some considerable time . . . The level we were assigned to work was 3000 feet below ground and over a mile in from the lift . . . The shaft was approximately 20 feet across with a height from floor to roof of seven feet. We were each supplied with a pit helmet and a miner's lamp. The day shift actually commenced at 7 am and finished at 5.30 pm. We were not given any food to consume during this time and we came to rely on our respective Polish workmate to provide us with a portion of his lunch packet. This inevitably consisted of pork fat sandwiches and a flask of ersatz coffee . . . We worked on the day shift for thirteen days at a time. On each alternate Sunday we had a rest day and then changed to the night shift. (For food) . . . we had a loaf of bread and pork fat spread in the early morning before the shift began. This was accompanied by a mug of mint tea. We drank half of this and used the remainder for shaving.

In the evening we were issued with the same amount of bread and, to go with it, a bowl of swede or fish soup . . . Red Cross parcels came to us from two different sources – England and Canada.[123]

Others among the POWs assigned to coal mining were not so sanguine:

I believed I had arrived in hell itself . . . The cavern was full of foul smoke. Pit props with flickering little lights on them leaned drunkenly out of the murk, and rows of naked black arms wielding shovels moved back and forth in the gloom. Above, a metal trough shook up and down, hurling lumps of coal back towards the conveyor belt and the noise of rock against metal, coupled with that of the compressed air engine was absolutely deafening.[124]

And, as always in mining, there was an ever-present threat of accident and injury:

Safety precautions below ground – especially where prisoners or slave workers were concerned – were minimal and gas inhalation as well as injury from unsafe equipment and roof-falls a constant danger. Men returning in a steady stream with smashed limbs and pulped faces were noted at Lamsdorf and most prisoners would have agreed with the assessment of the International Red Cross that the worst conditions, for working POWs, were to be found in the German mining industry.[125]

Königshütte Ostfeld, Chorzów – the Colliery where Dad worked underground for two and a half years.

12

YEARS TWO AND THREE OF
CAPTIVITY

D AD WORKED DOWN the mine near *Ligota* through the spring and early summer of 1941 but on Friday 4 July 1941 he was admitted to a hospital in *Katowice* suffering from a skin ulcer.[126] This must have been a significant lesion if it required in-patient treatment. The records relate that it was on the left side of the body but are not more specific. Perhaps it was on the leg, in which case it could have been a consequence of a wound that he had sustained under fire at *Cassel* or in trying to evade the enemy and reach *Dunkirk*. He was back at the mine on Friday 18 July 1941 and worked there for a further 21 months.[127]

Then, on Monday 19 April 1943, he had to report sick having injured his right hand.[128] His X-ray shows a badly displaced fracture of the right little finger. Work injuries are common in mining but there are reports of POWs becoming so exhausted and demoralised with their slavery that, in their desperation, they inflicted injuries on themselves ('*krankers*') in order to have a break from the work or, hopefully, be transferred to another occupation.[129] There is no means of knowing, now, the cause of Dad's injury but, with what would have been a heavily strapped hand, he was transferred back to *Stalag* on Wednesday 12 May 1943.[130]

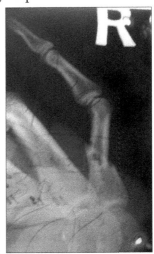

X-ray of Dad's right hand, 19 April 1943.

Whilst back at *Stalag* Dad would have noticed significant changes. He now had the benefit of the surprisingly good medical services that had been developed at the camp infirmary, despite all the predictable difficulties. The camp itself was now much larger with a new compound and huts for shot-down RAF aircrew (who were not sent out to work) but the intrinsic and pervasive miseries of overcrowded captivity remained. In general, the men confined to camp had become listless and irritable despite the regular Red Cross parcels and organised games and activities. Some had become 'sack-hounds', rising from their bunks only when forced. At this stage of the war there seemed no serious prospect of it ever ending and there was an air of tetchy gloom. Aggressive outbursts were common and 'barbed-wire fever' became so acute in some men that their irrational behaviour put them in danger.[131] Attacking a guard or throwing oneself at the wire fencing in frustration and being shot was effectively a form of suicide.

As a rule, communications with home were now well-established but here, too, there could be problems. The postbag could deliver a bombshell in the form of a 'Dear John' letter (as they were called) breaking off a relationship.[132] Birthdays and anniversaries could be particularly painful even when loyalties seemed secure. Prisoners also suffered a shared concern that those at home were failing to read between the lines of the obligatory cheerful missives sent off to the UK. POWs strongly suspected that their relatives didn't understand how drab, pointless and monotonous their wasted youthful lives really were. Even the photographs of smiling prisoners arranged in groups as sanctioned by the Germans were a 1940s version of 'fake news'. Men who opted for the offer of joining a group photograph were loaned new uniforms and decent boots to wear for the camera only to have to change back, afterwards, into their motley, threadbare and lousy rags and clogs.[133] They then shuffled back to their huts, accommodation that they now shared with fleas, lice, bed bugs, cockroaches, mice and rats.[134] Long hours could be wasted by POWs trying to free their clothing from the lice that hid in every tuck and seam and there was no possible way of reducing the insect population in the straw-filled palliasses on their beds. They all knew, by now, that their insanitary conditions and the widespread infestation they suffered could easily lead to an outbreak of typhus and rapid death.[135] They therefore felt it safer, however uncomfortable, to abandon their mattresses and sleep on bare boards. Not that many had a full quota – alternate ones were often missing after being used to fuel the hut stove over winter.[136] But despite all the desolation and despair, it was obvious to the Allied POWs that their lot could have been much worse.

OTHER PRISONERS

ONE DAY IN 1943 the Germans set up a barbed wire fence around a large open space just beyond the perimeter wire of *Stalag VIIB*. This created some interest and speculation among the British POWs and the intrigue was solved as they watched a long column of Russian POWs hobble into the new 'cage'.

(They were) . . . straggling columns of small, stocky young men in ragged olive-green uniforms bent with fatigue, their faces gaunt and grimed as they dragged themselves along, almost oblivious of their surroundings. They were marching Zombies.[137]

More and more columns arrived until there were many thousands of them. They had no shelter from the elements and simply lay on the grass. The British POWs saw the obvious distress and, with the Germans showing no inclination to offer the desperate Russians any food or drink, the 'Tommies' began to throw food scraps

Russian Prisoners of War in Germany. With no supply of Red Cross Parcels vast numbers starved to death. (Wikimedia Commons. Bundesarchiv).

and cigarettes over the wire. The German guards soon intervened and fired warning shots. It was very distressing for the British prisoners to have to witness such inhumanity and then see, each morning, the living Russians dragging their dead into pits they had been made to dig. This went on for some two weeks until the surviving Russians were marched away. In fact, the Germans had built a special camp for Russian prisoners in the middle of dense woodland only a few miles away from *Stalag VIIB* and it was estimated, after the war and after sample exhumations, that some 40,000 Russian POWs had died there and been thrown into mass graves. There is a large memorial at the site today in commemoration of the vast numbers of dead Russians who were systematically annihilated.[138]

Eventually, there were over 700 British work parties sent out from *Stalag VIIB* (and its extension from 1943) and the labouring encounters of any one prisoner could vary enormously. However, there were common experiences. And when passing through the main camp in transit from one *Arbeitskommando* to the next because the work had ceased or because of injury or illness, men inevitably compared notes. Some experiences, whether suffered directly or acquired by report, were not easily forgotten. The men were learning, all the time, more and more about the horrific regime of which they found themselves part.

Many work parties laboured alongside prisoners from other nations and one's neighbour at a workbench could be a political prisoner or a Jew from a concentration camp. In these situations the POWs learned that they were relatively fortunate, however abject their own daily lives. Concentration camp victims, their identity numbers tattooed on their arms and suffering the cold in their inadequate striped uniforms were worked and starved to death. If they collapsed they were beaten until the guards were satisfied that their frailty was genuine and that they were unlikely to contribute further to the economy of the Reich. They were then likely to be shot in full view of those around them.[139] They survived, if at all, on scraps of food they could scrounge or steal and, of course, never received Red Cross parcels. Allied POWs were, unavoidably, witnesses to this brutality but put themselves in danger if they obeyed their instincts and tried to intervene.

. . . the most wretched of all Hitler's slaves [were[the concentration camp inmates. Unlike the prisoners [of war] they had no Red Cross parcels and no one to complain to . . . their existence was a living death, the sight of which drove many of the POWs to despair. They watched the concentration camp inmates in their striped pyjamas grow weaker day by day. They watched them beaten and killed. They had no choice but to stand aside and watch the physical abuse of the old and weak, knowing they could do nothing to save them. Intervening to stop a beating would not save the victim, but it might cost the life of the POW.[140]

Concentration camp victims used as forced labour – here moving earth. (Wikimedia Commons. Bundesarchiv)

The unavoidable horror and helplessness were extremely stressful for Allied POWs when it was risky to show even the slightest humanitarian gesture such as slipping a concentration camp victim the stub of a cigarette or a morsel of food. But there was worse. When several work parties were sent, in October 1943,[141] to help build a factory complex near the town of *Auschwitz* (*Oświęcim* in Polish) they frequently noticed a sickly smell in the air.[142] By this time in the war it was common knowledge among the POWs that the Germans weren't above mass murder of innocent people. Now the men at *Stalag VIIIB* realised that the extermination process itself had become industrialised. Men, women and children arriving at *Auschwitz* in family groups were being cruelly separated. Some were being gassed immediately and then cremated in large ovens. Others, who appeared strong enough, were taken off and worked to death. Allied POWs at *Stalag VIIIB*, among others, were also aware that Russian POWs were also being treated as disposable. It was difficult for the POWs to avoid speculating that, as time passed and if the war looked lost, the Germans would not extend their slaughter to include anyone no longer fit to work. By 1943 many of the long-incarcerated Allied POWs had begun to think that their future was hardly worth living for, that their daily struggles and frustrations were pointless.

13
YEAR FOUR OF CAPTIVITY

A MONTH AFTER being returned to *Stalag* with his injured hand Dad was fully restored. He learned that he was not going back to the mine but out to another work party (E3) at *Blechhammer*, a synthetic oil plant near *Koźle* (*Cozel*) about 40 miles to the east of *Lambinowice*.[143] His job was to be painting but he would probably have been relieved to know that it was anything above ground. But *Blechhammer* was far from a pleasant place to work.[144] Prisoner accommodation, a collection of primitive wooden huts, was located alongside other similar camps about three-quarters of a mile from the actual factory. The food supplied was of the lowest quality; there was no running water and there were no proper toilets. Of the other camps in the complex, some were for Jewish slave labourers sent from *Auschwitz* and even though the conditions in which they lived and worked were abysmal, the Germans made no attempt to conceal them. There had been a typhus outbreak shortly after the camp was first opened in 1942 and of the 5,500 forced labourers brought to what was effectively an outpost of *Auschwitz* (60 miles to the east) over the next three years, a third of them would die there. Many were simply starved and worked to death and others succumbed to dysentery or tuberculosis.

It's perhaps no surprise, then, that Dad became ill. In mid-October 1943 he developed gastritis and, failing to improve, was transferred back to *Stalag* again on Monday 6 December.[145] Rest and a slightly better diet brought about little improvement and on Friday 28 January 1944 he began an intensive week's treatment in the hospital ward at *Stalag VIIIB*.[146]

He must have recovered well after that and on Friday 10 March 1944 he arrived at his next workplace (E367) – a sawmill at *Jägerndorf*, 30 miles south of *Lambinowice*.[147] His journey there had taken him across what had formerly been a national border into the former Czechoslovakian region of Moravia. *Jägerndorf* was the German name given to the Czech frontier town of *Krnov*. The town is adjacent to an extensive forested area as the land to the west rises into the *Jeseníky* mountain range and the 70 POWs employed at the sawmill were used, mostly, to load the logs and sawn timber for transportation.

14
YEAR FIVE OF CAPTIVITY

O N Sunday 2 July 1944 Dad was heading into his fifth year as a captive and slave and was transferred to another work party – E 782 – in *Kuźnia Raciborska (Ratiborhammer* in German) which was in the administrative area of the city of *Opava* (German *Troppau*).[148] *Opava* is also in present-day Czech Republic but *Kuźnia Raciborska* is just north

Allied POWs at forestry work (Wikimedia Commons. IWM).

of the border into present-day Poland. There is no clear indication of the type of work that Dad was forced to do but his new location was again on the edge of a forested area so he may have been doing similar work to that at *Krnov,* and his completed repatriation questionnaire relates that he worked at a sawmill both in 1944 *and* in 1945.[149]

CZECHOSLOVAK RESISTANCE

THE FACT THAT Dad's last two work parties were situated in (or virtually in) former Czechoslovak territory and among Czech people appears to be highly relevant to future events in his story. Despite the so-called 'Munich Agreement' of September 1938 giving Hitler the German-speaking border areas of the country he defiantly invaded the rest of Czechoslovakia only six months later.[150] Under German occupation – ruthless as elsewhere – there was very harsh rationing and many of the population were deported to Germany as forced labourers. There was even more suppression of freedoms after Reinhardt Heydrich was sent to Prague in September 1941 to further enforce the Nazi regime.[151] But even in the face of the brutally repressive activities of the Gestapo the Czech population refused to cower. There was widespread non-cooperation in industry and secret resistance cells emerged, some declaring allegiance to their exiled government and some loyal to Stalin and communism. After one resistance group assassinated Heydrich in May 1942 there were appalling reprisals and on a massive scale. The degree of hatred of the Germans shared by most Czechs became deeply entrenched and as the war progressed a strong resistance infrastructure developed. By 1945 there were many partisan groups hounding the Germans.[152] Allied POWs, particularly those working among the native Czech population, couldn't be but aware of the loathing and hostility towards the Nazi intruders and of the existence of resistance fighters. It was useful insight when their future was so insecure.

The early depredations suffered by the POWs arriving at Stalag VIIIB (and at other camps) in 1940 had been somewhat relieved by the appearance of regular Red Cross parcels and by new uniforms and boots. The food parcels continued to arrive over the next four years, effectively keeping the men alive, and there were consignments of sundries from other charities. Further replacement uniforms were not so reliably distributed, however, and by 1944 most of the POWs were wearing makeshift and closely repaired clothing that had once been the uniforms of any number of continental armies.[153] This was, though, the year that brought encouraging news – D-Day. In fact, thanks to the now widespread use of illicit radio sets ('canaries'), many Allied POWs knew of the 6 June invasion of mainland Europe before their guards, an interesting inversion of locus of control.

There was now some prospect that the war would be brought to a conclusion as fighting fronts were steadily reducing the extent of the 'Reich'. At the same time there was now an increasing danger of collateral damage from Allied bombing raids. Men on work parties at large industrial plants, especially those producing artificial fuels, were at particular risk[154] and the Germans provided no air raid shelters for prisoner labourers. In the latter half of 1944 over 700 British and Commonwealth POWs in Europe were killed in Allied air raids.[155] It was safer to be back at *Stalag* even though prevailing conditions there were declining. Overcrowding and insect infestation were at their peaks, intensifying the claustrophobia, and the men were finding it more and more difficult to maintain morale. Bar the most recent arrivals, the men were thin and apathetic and there had been deaths from typhus, a rapidly fatal infection spread by lice.[156] Most of the living now had the symptoms and signs of prolonged vitamin deficiencies with no prospect of improvement.[157] Indeed, the dispersal of Red Cross parcels was beginning to break down (more and more were disappearing into the German black market)[158] and the appalling rations issued by the Germans had deteriorated further. The erratic arrival of Red Cross parcels also interrupted the supply of cigarettes, and a craving for nicotine, a chemical antidote to hunger, made many dejected men wretched.[159] But things were getting desperate throughout the shrinking territories of the *Reich*.

By the spring of 1945, many Allied POWs in Germany were starving, the distribution of Red Cross Parcels having collapsed or subverted to the 'black market'. (Wikimedia Commons).

THE GERMAN COLLAPSE

B Y THE BEGINNING of 1945 it was difficult to see how Germany could expect any outcome of the war other than defeat. The nation's three major industrial regions – the Ruhr, the Saar and Silesia – lay in the shadow of the guns of either the western Allies or of the Russians. By 14 January the German surprise armour-led counterattack in the *Ardennes* – an intended drive to the Belgian coast at *Antwerp* and so divide the

Allied armies in the west – had clearly failed. The Germans were trying to withdraw their forces in an organised way but were continually harried by the Americans and British despite the bitterly cold, foggy weather and repeated snow blizzards. And so, by mid-January, it was clear that Germany would soon be fighting only on its own territory. Moreover, it was obvious that it was tottering economically. Thanks to the Allied air offensive against fuel refineries and transportation during the summer/autumn of 1944, shipment of coal across Germany had fallen by two thirds and the production of synthetic fuels by more than 90 per cent.[160] The next six weeks – late January and February 1945, as a spring thaw began – saw the Allies in the west push the Germans back to the *River Rhine* and even take an intact rail bridge (at *Remagen*) across the river on 7 March.[161]

By the end of March 1945, Germany as a nation state had virtually ceased to exist. The fuel situation was desperate, many towns and cities, especially in the industrial areas, had been bombed nearly out of existence, and with vast numbers, civilian and military personnel alike, fleeing in front of the Russian advances to the east, there were some 10 million refugees on the move. Among them were slave labourers, concentration camp victims, and Allied POWs whose camps in East Prussia, Poland and some of Czechoslovakia had already been overrun by the Red Army. But there were still no signs of a German surrender. Once it was clear that the natural defence lines of the *Rhine* and the *Oder* had been breached, the remaining effective *Nazi* military units had been withdrawn into separate components around important towns and cities. However, there was still a rumour (actually unfounded) of the *Nazis* retreating to a 'redoubt' in the *Harz* mountains in the centre of Germany in order to fight to the death – the '*Götterdämmerung*' scenario.[162]

The last week of March 1945 also saw the strategic planning, by the Allies, of the final stages to victory. With the Russians already within reach of *Berlin*, the original scheme – a single powerful thrust on the German capital once the industrial *Ruhr* 'pocket' had been encircled and isolated – was abandoned. It was replaced by a broad front advance by the British and American armies until they reached the line of the River *Elbe*. This runs southeast to northwest across the centre of Germany from above *Leipzig* to near *Hamburg* and gave a natural dividing line between, and target for, the western and eastern combatants.[163] Some days the Allies made rapid, almost unopposed progress but on other

occasions there was still bitter and costly fighting. *Ehrfurt* was taken on
11 April,[164] *Weimar* early on the 12th and American units reached the
Elbe near *Magdeburg* later that day (they came across Russian units near
Torgau on the 25th). *Leipzig* fell on 19 April and all the time the Russians
were closing on the very centre of *Berlin*. *Nuremberg*, which had great
symbolic relevance for the *Nazis*, fell on 20 April, General *Patton* reached
Chemnitz on the 25th and five days later, with close fighting going on in
the very streets above his bunker in *Berlin*, *Hitler* committed suicide.
The inevitable end of the *Third Reich* was a week later.

As Allied troops progressed across German homeland, they made
many discoveries; some of them horrifying. The first concentration
camp overrun was on 4 April – at *Ohrdruf* near *Erfurt* by an American
armoured unit.[165] A larger camp was discovered at *Nordhausen* between
Hamburg and *Leipzig* on 11 April as well as underground factories
manned by starving slave labourers. Initial shock and revulsion soon
turned into determination to finish all German resistance as quickly as
possible. Other discoveries included Allied POW camps, and the first
of many large compounds – at *Hammelburg* between *Frankfurt* and
Bamberg – was opened on 6 April.

Perhaps the most historically significant event of this late stage
of the war was the meeting of American and Russian troops along the
banks of the *River Elbe* near *Torgau* during the afternoon of 25 April.[166]
Now the end was certain:

*The German state had disintegrated. Where once there was strict compliance
and firm discipline with everything functioning efficiently, now there was
total disorder and anarchy. It was as though a hoop had been knocked off a
barrel, causing all the staves to collapse. There was no central government,
no local authorities, and the Burgomeister under arrest. Banks, post-offices
and schools were all shut. The trains had come to a standstill. Thousands
were on the move – German soldiers and family groups who had escaped the
Russian advance, and slave labourers from every country in Europe and Asia,
liberated from their camps.*[167]

15
THE BEGINNING OF THE END

THE DEATH MARCH AND ESCAPE

Long before the 'Armageddon' of late spring 1945 there had been dark clouds accumulating over the well-being of all the Allied POWs and they had deep fears for their immediate future. The Germans might still organise a successful counterattack on one or all of the fronts, or a dogged defence of their 'Fatherland' could lapse into a military stalemate. The war might go on and on and on. And if the German economy continued to slide – as it was obviously doing – POWs could come to be seen as an unnecessary drain on resources. They might be used as human shields in combat or simply exterminated alongside any remaining Jews.[168] There was even a strong belief that *Hitler* was planning to have all prisoners of war shot if the Allies did not stop bombing Germany. The latest gossip – over Christmas 1944 – came almost as a relief: that those POWs nearest the advancing Russian front, at the camps in former Poland, were to be moved westward into Germany. Few, however, suspected that they would be force-marched on virtually no food or drink and through the coldest winter since 1940.

The term 'death march' should be in the plural. There were many such enforced evacuations from the eastern areas of the greater *Nazi Reich* during late 1944 and the first months of 1945. There were, across territories that had formerly been Poland, Romania, Czechoslovakia, the Baltic States, and others, many hundreds of thousands of work camp prisoners (estimates average 700,000) – many Jews and others in concentration camps and extermination camps and Allied prisoners of war (many Russian) in POW camps.

Streams of people were winding through the wreckage of Germany in those final months of the war. German refugees, slave labourers, concentration-camp inmates and prisoners of war of every nationality flowed westward in the cold and the damp, bedding down where they could, living off the land – or what was left of it by now. Life was cheap . . . it seemed that half the world was on the move . . . central Europe was a seething mass of the dispossessed.[169]

Himmler had ordered, on 17 June, 1944, that no living captives (of any type) were to fall into enemy hands if the boundaries of the *Greater Reich* receded. According to his order all District SS Commanders were empowered, in the face of 'emergency conditions', to determine the fate of all camps and inmates under their jurisdiction. In the eventuality, as the American, British and Russian armies made very significant advances during and after summer 1944, there was confusion and inconsistency regarding the evacuation of Germany's prisoners. Many camp commandants waited anxiously until things were desperate in the hope of more explicit orders from on high. In some instances, low-ranking *Nazis* used their broad mandate to murder prisoners who were not fit for evacuation and in some places even those who were.[170] After that the prisoners, on what some called the 'frostbite marches' and others the 'death marches', found themselves at the mercy of the guards appointed to shepherd them west.

In January 1945 there were some 40,000 guards serving the *Reich* at camps (of all kinds) in the eastern ranges of the 'Fatherland'.[171] From their accounts after the war, it's clear that, from the moment marching columns left their camps, the guards were abandoned to their own fates as much as their charges. The guards themselves were left to trek along in the terrible weather with their prisoners, trying to find them some sustenance and water, and trying to stop them escaping. Both guards and prisoners were led to believe that they were heading for rail heads where they would board trains but only to find, time and again, that the trains did not materialise – that they had been delayed or destroyed by Allied air raids or commandeered for military purposes. Many of the dismal columns of humanity covered hundreds of miles, travelling up to three months. It is no surprise that the disillusioned guards became intolerant, irrational and trigger-happy. They came to see their charges as holding them back from their own desires to hurry west and avoid capture by the Russians. It is estimated that at least a third of the prisoners (of all kinds) evacuated did not survive. The 'death marches' suffered by some 80,000 Allied prisoners of war who had been incarcerated in *Stalags* and their work-party satellites in the east of the *Reich* should be seen in all this context. A greater proportion of them survived than did the concentration camp victims or Russian prisoners of war. However, this should not distract from the abominable suffering they had to endure. Among the marchers were a few prisoners who were qualified doctors and one of them recorded his observations immediately after the war:

Hundreds of the men suffered from malnutrition, exposure, trench foot, exhaustion, dysentery, tuberculosis and other diseases. So little water was issued to us that men drank water or snow from the ground or from ditches that others had used as latrines. Men collapsed from hunger, fear, malnutrition, exhaustion, or disease. Many marched along with large abscesses on their feet. Mud and cold brought frostbite and even gangrene and amputation. I personally slept beside men suffering from Erysipelas, Diphtheria, Pneumonia, Malaria and other diseases. Dysentery was so common and so severe that wherever our column went, there was a trail of bloody movements and discarded underwear (which was sorely needed for warmth).[172]

It was certainly poor consolation but the Allied POWs could, at least, be relieved that their situation was not so appalling as that of the columns of concentration camp victims or Russian POWs that they happened to pass. The Germans had come to believe that these charges were members of inferior races and therefore subhuman ('*Untermenschen*') and destined, anyway, to extermination by starvation or by being worked to death.

A thousand, maybe two thousand, people were standing beside the road, having been made to wait for us to overtake them because they were slower than us. They were in blue and white striped pyjama-type clothes and wearing big clogs. They had no overcoats. They were from Auschwitz . . . not too far from where we had come. As we slowly moved by them, I looked at their faces. I looked in vain for a vestige, a flicker of human interest, of recognition, a hint of understanding, anything in their faces showing they were aware of us or anything. There was nothing. The treatment, the weather, had sucked the life out of them. They stood like zombies on the roadside. Their heads like skulls, their eyes large, luminous and staring, all the same, not a flicker of feeling, like dead men but still alive.[173]

SILESIA IN OUR STORY

In order to understand in detail what Dad actually experienced on his particular 'death march' we are able to refer to a verbatim diary written up daily throughout one of the many marches, indeed one that took virtually the same route to Germany as Dad was compelled to do. Private George Kear (GK), a native of *Pillowell*, near *Lydney* in Gloucestershire, was a member of the 5th Battalion of the Gloucestershire Regiment (no. 5185934).* He had been captured during the retreat from Belgium in May 1940 and he, also, had endured a horrific journey to *Lamsdorf* (prisoner no. 10346) and had spent five years slaving in German industry, latterly in a sugar beet processing plant at *Bauerwitz (Baborów)*. The factory was about 40 miles southeast of *Stalag VIIIB* and was also very close to the pre-occupation border between Poland and Czechoslovakia. In his diary for 1945 GK's daily entries relate how and where the groups of Allied POWs in his vicinity (mostly men out of camp on work parties) were congregated and then assembled into columns, each of about 1,000 men. He then records, for each day that late winter and spring, the overnight stop locations (the German names given to Czech villages and towns along the route) and the conditions they encountered. The prisoners from parties working to the south and east of *Lamsdorf* were not taken back to *Stalag* but put on a route that took them through northern Czechoslovakia, as GK's diary confirms.

Dad was still with the work party (E782) at *Kuźnia Raciborska* in late January 1945 when the men were escorted away to join the columns

*   In fact, GK had kept daily diaries throughout much of his captivity and generously allowed me to access them before he died in 2013.

of POWs being force-marched away to the south west, away from the advancing Russians.[174] The Red Army took *Gliwice* on Wednesday 24 January.[175] GK reports, in his diary, that on Thursday 25 January,

Two or three parties of English boys come through from Gliwitz (Gliwice) and Beuthen (Bytom) – been on the way three or four days.

The most direct route from *Gliwice* and *Bytom* to *Baborów (Bauerwitz),* where GK was still working in the sugar beet factory, is via the *Kuźnia Raciborska* area. GK also reports meeting other parties of English POWs, that had been force-marched from *Bytom,* on Thursday 25 January. In other words, there is strong circumstantial evidence that Dad and his E782 workmates would have been ordered away from their workplace and into one of these marching columns during the week beginning Monday 22 January 1945.

The POWs in *Stalag VIIIB* itself were warned that they would be leaving – with two hours' notice – during the afternoon of 22 January and were marched out of the camp at 6pm. It was, of course, already dark, there was a snow blizzard and the air temperature was already well below freezing. They were force-marched west, without any significant rest stops, for the next 28 hours, covering 29 kilometres. The POWs in the hospital and those just too unwell to march were abandoned to their fate – to the Russians. In releasing their emotions, the prisoners took delight in burning down substantial parts of the camp over the next few days.[176]

George Kear's group set off from their secure camp near the sugar refinery at *Baborów,* where they worked, on Friday 26 January 1945. They marched due west, on side roads, to *Pietrowice,* which is just north of the town of *Krnov.* Having arrived on 28 January they were billeted there, under guard, for a week; a week in which GK describes the weather as bitterly cold. During that time other groups of prisoners who had been on work parties (some more from *Bytom,* for instance) joined them. There appears to have been an organised procedure in which men from work parties were brought to assembly points before being set off to march west away from the advancing Russians. On Tuesday 30 January three columns of men were assembled and marched away down the road to the south, through *Krnov,* in the first instance. George Kear's column followed them on Monday 5 February.

The marching columns appear to have followed a common route for GK refers, severally, to the conditions of their overnight billets being very dependent on the previous night's occupants. The men learned to dread, especially, being next behind a column of Russian prisoners for they always left the overnight stops in a filthy state and heavily contaminated by lice. They also hoped, throughout each exhausting day, that there would be food made available at night stops but very often there was none. GK records that local inhabitants sometimes appeared with bread and other items, which the guards allowed them to distribute, but there was never enough to go around. The men assuaged their thirst by melting snow but this was nearly always soiled and there were soon cases of dysentery.

On Tuesday 6 February George Kear's column were marching through the town of *Bruntál* in the *Jeseníky* mountains, having climbed up to an elevation of 1,300 feet. The prevailing weather was snow mixed with hail. After four days more of constant daylight marching through snow and slush the column arrived at *Šumperk (Schönberg)*. So far, they had marched about 100 miles. Thus, we can assume that the column in which Dad was being force-marched would also have been well into Czechoslovak territory by the middle of February 1945; heading west somewhere in or just beyond the *Jeseníky* mountains. George Kear reports men going missing on occasions – for instance, during the night stop of 26/27 February when three POWs fled during darkness.

Dad and a friend, Frederick Lloyd Randall, were two of such fugitives. Their bid for freedom must have been somewhere in the vicinity of *Šumperk* and sometime between 5 and 15 February 1945. Corporal Frederick 'Lloyd' Randall (5182445), from Woolstone near Cheltenham, was also of the Gloucestershire Regiment, and also of the Second Battalion. He had enlisted as a private (for seven years) in the 'Glosters' on 25 September 1934, at the age of 21.[177] This was just a few months before Dad had enlisted, and Lloyd and Ron became friends. Although from different basic training cohorts, they were 'thrown together' when they were both detached to *Aldershot* in late November 1935 to attend a driving and vehicle mechanics course. Issued with provisional driving licences, the two young soldiers learnt to drive and how to keep their vehicles functioning and roadworthy. A few months later they travelled, with the rest of their Battalion, to *Alexandria* when the Italian invasion of Libya appeared to be a threat to the British interests in Egypt.

Dad and Lloyd both remained with the Second Battalion until and into the war. There is good visual evidence of their shared common experiences – compare the photograph below with that of Dad on

5182445 Frederick Lloyd Randall, Gloucestershire Regiment, about 1938. Note the similarity with the frontispiece, especially the bundle of clothing folded on the running board of the lorry. (He also features in the group on p.13 – second right). (Randall/Bird family)

frontispiece, noting especially the article strapped to the running board in both images. More strongly binding in friendship would have been that they saw action together in France. They both fought at *Cassel* but Corporal Randall was wounded during the fighting of Wednesday 29 May 1940 and taken into captivity by the Germans that day. He was transported to the nearest large town – *St. Omer.* He had been injured in the lower back or buttock; probably a penetrating shrapnel wound (he was known to suffer, life-long, a deep, draining sinus in that part of the body).

His wound was treated in a hospital in *St. Omer:* he appears to have received good care from the German (or French) clinical staff there. When suitably recovered he was transferred to a prison camp in Germany – initially to *Stalag 5B.* This camp was in the *Black Forest* area near the town of *Villingen,* some 70 miles south of Stuttgart. He was later moved, on 14 March 1941, to another POW camp – to *Stalag 21A* – which was between *Hamburg* and *Rostock.* He was incarcerated at this larger camp for just over a year before being moved again. This time he was sent even further east, travelling to *Stalag VIIIB* in *Silesia* on 14 May 1942. At *Lamsdorf* he was obliged to go out on work parties, as were all ranks under Sergeant, and although his German work record card has not been found, he himself reports[178] having worked at a logging camp and sawmill near the town of *Krnov (Jägerndorf* in German) across the border in Czechoslovakia. This was exactly where Dad worked between March and July 1944 and the two men may have been able to rekindle their friendship at this time. They were certainly in the same 'death march' column when they were put on the roads through northern Czechoslovakia in late January 1945 and the remainder of this story is one of their joint escape, shared existence in hiding, and journey back to England and home.

Dad and Lloyd both knew, from their contacts with locals on work parties, that the attitude of many of the Czech nationals towards them was very sympathetic – as friendly, indeed, as was, on the other hand, the Czech's intense hatred of the Germans. The two POWs presumably hoped that they could obtain help and support of some partisans or resistance fighters if not from among the local population. On the other hand, Dad certainly knew that the Germans would be unrelenting towards the men on the marches and force them on to the point of exhaustion, starvation and near-death without scruple – he had experienced this in northern France and Belgium in 1940. And since 1940 the utter brutality of the *Nazi* regime had become totally institutionalised. Nonetheless the two prisoners were taking a supreme gamble – they could not have known how much, if any, help they were going to receive. It could have led to disaster – declaring themselves to *Sudeten* Germans or other *Nazi* sympathisers would have been the end of their venture – perhaps a fatal one. But it would have been very clear to them that continuing the march also had a high risk of mortality. Quite how they got free, whether it was planned, or a sudden opportunity taken on impulse, cannot now be known. Nor do we know whether it was at night or during a day's march. A captured RAF airman on a very similar march further north in Poland has described his bolt for freedom. Though he was soon recaptured he illustrates the sort of circumstances that gave rise to men risking an escape:

The goons [guards] endeavoured to regulate the marching columns to ensure that they got to a farm an hour or so before dark. This would give them time to count heads and dole out any bread ration before everyone was locked away in a barn or similar building for the night. It was a week (later) that the Germans miscalculated and it was dark by the time we reached the farm for our overnight stay. We left the road and started down a narrow farm track which had a hedgerow on one side and deep snowdrifts covering the verges. We still had about 200 yards to go to reach the farm buildings when I noticed a gap in the hedge on the far side of the nearest goon . . . Checking once more that we were nowhere near a guard, I darted through the gap in the hedge and dived headlong into a snowdrift . . . I dared not move until the column had passed by for fear of presenting a silhouette against the snow for the goons to shoot. As I lay cocooned in the snowdrift I experienced a fear of what would happen to me should I be recaptured and, at the same time, a certain elation that with luck I would soon meet up with the Red Army and be homeward bound.[79]

16
ESCAPE AND INTO HIDING IN BRNÍČKO*

Howsoever it was that Dad and Lloyd Randall managed to escape, they probably backtracked at first. Returning along the previous day's trek through the slurry of mud and slush would have hidden their footprints. It was too easy for the Germans to follow a track in virgin snow, even at night. But after a reasonable distance the two men must have turned south. After (we guess) some five to ten miles of a night-

The village of Brníčko in Moravia, Czech Republic in 2017.

* The events recorded in this section are the result of having met descendants of Jan and Anna Weinlich (see below) and of their amazing hospitality and cooperation.

time hike they came to the edge of a village. Perhaps they lurked in the woods and watched to assess their prospects; we don't know. More likely, in their frozen and famished state, they would have been impelled to take a desperate chance and knock at the first door they came to. But whatever the circumstances of the meeting, the two men had walked into the lives of the *Weinlich* family in *Brníčko* (pronounced *Brewnishko*).

The home of the *Weinlich* family was a long, low, tripartite building near the northern margin of the Czech village. Descendants still live in the premises. In February 1945 *Jan Weinlich* was aged 46 and his wife, *Anna*, 47. They had a daughter, *Emilie* (then aged 18), and a son, *Jan* (aged 16), both still living at home. Jan senior was a smallholder with a few farm animals. Hunting and exploiting the forests brought the family further sustenance and fuel. In the harsh winters of central Europe the livestock were brought in from their pastures – to the central section of the house – and were fed from the forage stored in the third part of the property.

No-one currently surviving in the *Weinlich* family has any knowledge of the nature of the arrival of Dad and Lloyd. It was customary, during winter, for local inhabitants to scour the nearby forests for firewood and on an almost daily basis. The initial meeting might, therefore, have been away from the *Weinlich* home but it is certainly the case that the two escapees were welcomed into the household to be revived. The *Weinlichs* were taking a huge risk. Revelation of their complicity to the local authorities would have resulted in the execution of the whole family. At a more mundane level they were going to have to cope with two men who were effectively destitute. By now the POWs on the death marches were all half-starved, physically derelict, dirty, lousy, and often carrying infectious diseases. Their

Jan and Anna Weinlich after the war. (Weinlich/Zajíček family).

uniforms were worn-out, their boots falling apart. They had no spare clothing and virtually no personal articles of hygiene. Dad and Lloyd would have been able, however, to make simple conversation in German and both men probably knew a little Czech. Their dog-tags proved their identity (though there could be no absolute certainty that they weren't 'agents provocateurs'). Despite all this the *Weinlichs* took the men in and they were to be part of the family for about a month!

The amazing generosity of the *Weinlich* family towards the two refugees is brought home when one considers its effect on their daily living, let alone the courage it took to put their own survival in such jeopardy. The two men would have brought with them virtually only the clothes they were wearing and a few, small, personal effects and documents. We know that Dad had his army pay-books, a photograph

of his mother, and a pocket edition of the New Testament that she had also sent out to him. Lloyd had a few photographs, some of himself when a lot younger and fitter.* If they had carried any food with them, it would have been a pitiable amount. Both men were smokers and probably almost as desperate for nicotine as they were hungry for food. If they weren't strikingly stubbly or bearded, they were certainly in need of some new razor blades and the attentions of a barber. Nonetheless, as long-serving regular soldiers who were well-adapted to a sparse, disciplined life, even before imprisonment, they were able to adapt quickly to the rigours imposed by hiding in a civilian household behind enemy lines.How grateful they would have been for comfortable, warm beds in a dry

The inscribed photograph (taken before the war) that Lloyd Randall left with the Weinlich family.

building but easily able to understand the need to restore their beds to an unused appearance early morning. They appreciated why they must

*   He gave one of these to the Weinlich family when he left, inscribing his name and home address in England on the rear. I found an exact match of this photograph (uninscribed) in my mother's effects when she died. When the Weinlich descendants sent me a digital copy of their photograph of Lloyd, that was when I knew that I had surely found the family who had hidden the two men and saved their lives.

not cross the yard to the privy in daylight and why they should keep away from the windows of the house. How they should always keep any tell-tale signs of their presence out of sight and why their places at the table at mealtimes were so transient. And, above all, they would have realised the absolute need for them to be prepared, at a moment's notice, to quickly slink away to a particular hiding place should their presence be in danger of revelation.

The Weinlich house in Brníčko - in which Dad and Lloyd were hidden (in the section behind the wheelie bin).

The two soldiers were accommodated in the house but if there was any risk of discovery – approaching police or Germans, for instance – they were hastened into the mid-section of the house that served as a winter stall for the animals. Here there was a large metal feeding trough which, if dragged to one side, revealed a hidden chamber beneath and the men would clamber down to lie quietly until it was safe to surface. Presumably there was no light and the confined space would have been cold even if some straw had been put down. It would also have been claustrophobic for the hidden men when they couldn't know what was happening above ground and for how long they might have to keep absolutely still and be confined. How many times the escapees had to submit to this precaution is not known but in a small community in which there were plenty of neighbours who could not be trusted, and where there was a regular German troop presence, it could have been a daily experience. The stress on everyone must have been cumulative. Although the ruse worked well, it might easily have been exposed and the story could have ended in tragedy.

Within a few days Dad and Lloyd would have gained enormously from being clean, dry, warm, fed a varied diet and having comfortable, regular sleep. They were able to appreciate what they had long lost – the pleasures of living with a family in a home. A sense of security and well-being is enormously recuperative. And, as they grew familiar with their surroundings, both men would have felt intuitively at home: the wooded hills and undulating fields around the village of *Brnícko* are very reminiscent of west Gloucestershire, of the hinterland of both *Woolaston* and *Woolstone*. The two men soon had the energy to want to help, to contribute to the household. They were probably given some simple tasks but there was no way in which they could compensate the *Weinlichs* for the extra food and clothing they needed, for the upsurge in washing and drying of clothes (in seclusion), and certainly not for the dangers they were causing. The two soldiers, long incarcerated, were probably mystified why the *Weinlich* family should be so assiduous towards them. They probably couldn't appreciate, at first, why most Czechs were so profoundly anti-German and why they were prepared to put themselves in such danger.

Dad and Lloyd would have known that the Czech population had felt betrayed by the outcome of the 1938 '*Munich* Crisis' and when neither the French nor British governments intervened to prevent Hitler's land grab and takeover of the rest of their country. They probably didn't know, however, about the murder of the *Reich Protector Heydrich*, in 1942, by some agents of the exiled Czech government in London. And they were very unlikely to have had any knowledge of the savage German reprisals – of the complete destruction of the Czech communities of *Lidice* and *Ležáky* after the mass executions of every male inhabitant and the deportations of all the women and children for extermination (some 1,300 people all told). It is small wonder that the Czech population were now so anti-German and prepared to act out their antagonism whatever the risks. The two escapees would also have learned, in this context, that other families in the locality had taken in escapees from the 'death march' columns. Among these was the *Zajíček* family destined, after the war, to become related to the *Weinlichs* by marriage. Moreover, Jan

Weinlich showed yet more courage and generosity later in the spring when he found a near-moribund Russian POW in the woods near his home and took him, also, under his wing until he had recovered. And, near a village about ten miles west, we know that the locals there hid some English airmen – who had baled out of their stricken bomber – in the cellars of a redundant factory, sustaining them for over a year before organising their repatriation.

Dad and Lloyd remained living with the *Weinlichs* for about a month. It must have seemed like heaven to them, however modest and austere the life of the family after five years of German occupation. The enlarged household had time to settle into a new routine that probably involved some common amusements and simple home entertainment such as card games. However, any humdrum was very brittle. One day a lorry carrying German troops was seen approaching the house. Dad and Lloyd were quickly dropped into their hiding place and covered over. The lorry drew up outside and one of the soldiers was seen to jump down with a sniffer dog on a lead. The present family don't know who but one of the *Weinlich* household had the presence of mind to push their cat through the door just as the dog-handler approached the building. The cat froze with fear on seeing the dog and then bolted. The dog, for his part, reacted fiercely and broke free of his master who watched, bemused and annoyed, as his animal chased after the cat, both at top speed. The German soldier shouted to his colleagues and they all ran after the animals, eventually into the woods. When they returned with their dog, some while later, they were all wet, cold and breathless. Weary and disgruntled, they just clambered back into their lorry and left. Doubtless the cat was given an extra saucer of milk that evening.

The Czech Republic remains in the grip of winter well into April, especially in the mountainous areas. Seasonal infection rates stay high and sometime whilst being hidden by the *Weinlich* family Dad contracted influenza. Someone in the family, or a trusted visitor, must have been the transmitter. As is typical, he developed a high temperature, a profound malaise and a strident cough. Because smoke from more than one chimney would have aroused suspicion in the village, the family were forced to nurse their guest under blankets in a cold bedroom. The cough resounded throughout the small house. Late one afternoon the village policeman (friendly on the face of it but almost certainly a puppet of the Germans) called at the house to invite himself to a game of cards; a regular occurrence. To have refused him hospitality would have been suspicious. *Jan Weinlich* sent for some neighbours to form a card school. But he also primed one of his most trusted friends to appear in the house wrapped in a blanket and with a pretend cough. The make-believe patient promptly excused himself from the card game and pretended to retire upstairs because of feeling so unwell. Thankfully, the ploy worked, nothing untoward was suspected and Dad was nursed to a full recovery.

There is a revealing parallel story of hiding a combatant from the Germans in a published memoir by a British Brigadier who escaped from hospital after being wounded at *Arnhem*. If he had been discovered it is certain, though he himself might have been re-imprisoned, that all the members of the household secreting him would have been shot or sent to concentration camps:

Searches were frequent in the town and were always possible . . . . The probability that our house too would at some time be searched grew with the passage of time. We worked out and practised a drill for my concealment, in a hiding place between the floor of the landing outside my bedroom and the ceiling of the hall below, and for the rapid removal of all traces of a compromising presence in the house. If a search happened at night one of the aunts would occupy my bed and act as a very sick woman. Another would help me to the hole, put the lid on after I was safely in and straighten up the carpet. A third would hold the enemy in conversation through the front door until all was ready. Everything that could knock a few seconds off our time for the whole manoeuvre was studied and every night before Miss Ann tucked me up she put anything in the way of English books or writing into a closet, together with odd things like English cigarettes, tobacco, male clothing and anything else likely to arouse suspicion in the room of a sick woman. All was hidden and enough clothes were set out for me, exactly arranged on a chair so placed that I could find it in the dark, to provide against the possibility of a prolonged search and a long cold spell for me in the hiding place.[180]

17
ACROSS CZECHOSLOVAKIA TO GERMANY AND FREEDOM

AFTER ABOUT A MONTH it was time for Dad and Lloyd to move on. After all, the object of their escape was to get back to England. Now, however, they had increased their chances of success to an enormous extent. They had recovered their strength and their health thanks to the *Weinlichs* and they were about to be offered more significant help, even beyond the extra clothing and replacement footwear that their journey would demand. One of the very few things that Dad ever revealed to his family before his death in 1980 was that it had been the Czech 'underground' that had got him through to the American lines and thence home. The implications of this bald statement were never really understood until, in recent months, contact has been made with the *Weinlich* family (by tracing backwards from a sliver of paper, recording their name and address, that was found among some photographs when the author's mother died in 1997 – see below). By about the middle of March 1945 *Jan Weinlich* must have arranged, through contacts in the vicinity, for his two guests to be taken in hand by local resistance and passed via their network towards and beyond *Prague* to the German border. In fact, the two fugitives may well have been united with other compatriots who had also been in hiding and a cohort of men escorted away. There must have been some intense emotions as the two refugees left their hiding place in *Brníčko* and there was an interchange of keepsakes. Dad returned to England with a slip of paper bearing the *Weinlich* family name and home address (in *Emilie's* handwriting) and a black and white postcard image of the village. Lloyd gave the *Weinlich* family a photograph of himself bearing his home address on the rear – probably one of the few valuable items he had in his possession. Indeed, there may have been more small gifts given and received but those mentioned, at least, have survived the decades.

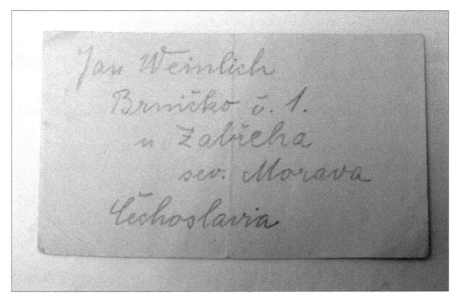

Slip of paper giving the Weinlich details. Dad must have secreted this about his person and brought it back to England. It is in the hand of the Weinlich daughter – Emilie.

By now it was increasingly clear that the German *Reich* was collapsing and that the Russian and the Western Allied fronts would soon meet and the war would be over. But until early May it was not safe to travel openly across Czechoslovakia. The name of the resistance guide in *Brníčko* was *František Kupka* who, ironically, lived directly opposite the village police station: the best place to hide has always been in the open! It was almost certainly *Mr. Kupka* who took the two POWs (perhaps more) off on the first leg of their journey home and would have handed them over to a trusted colleague after a few miles, and from this meeting they would have been taken on to some sort of safe house or refuge to rest. The same relay process would have occurred regularly, probably daily, as the two men trekked west. By now winter was passing and there must have been times when the two escapees revelled in their freedom, their continuing support, and in some spring sunshine glowing in the attractive countryside. Indeed, rural Czechoslovakia would have reminded them of their boyhoods in the Severn valley. There was always, however, an anxiety that they might stumble into a German patrol or that they might be betrayed by someone. From *Brníčko* the German border is some 300 miles as the crow flies. Dad and Lloyd needed to cover more ground than the proverbial corvid, however, for they would have been led along indirect and remote forest tracks and on large detours around towns and villages. Unless part of their journey was by train (by road vehicle seems highly unlikely), and allowing that they may have been walking at night and taking some rest days, they probably covered nearer 400 miles in, say, about six or seven weeks. This would have brought them to the newly liberated area of south-east Germany sometime in the first two weeks of May. *Bayreuth* had been taken by the Americans on 14 April and *Nuremberg* on the 20th – the two large German cities nearest to the western Czechoslovak border.[181]

'Operation Exodus' – Allied POWs preparing to board converted Lancaster bombers for the final leg of their flight home, April and May 1945.
(Wikimedia Commons).

It was on 6 May 1945 that Dad and Lloyd were, effectively, freed. Lloyd reports, in his POW repatriation questionnaire, completed when back in England,[182] that it was on that day that the Czech underground guide or guides handed the men over 'into Russian hands' on the outskirts of the Czech border town of *Děčín* (pronounced Dehsheen). The town is on the east bank of the *River Elbe* which served, during these times, as the demarcation line between Russian-held territory and that part of the dying *Reich* held by the Allies (here Americans). Fortunately, the Red Army unit did not decide to detain the men and it was a short journey across the river, by bridge or boat, that took them to freedom. Dad and Lloyd were now in the hands of the Americans and one step further towards absolute liberty, but still far from home. They were detained somewhere in Germany for the next fortnight and probably glad to eat decent food and to rest. They were probably surprised, however, how quickly they were then filtered into what had rapidly developed into a well-organised system for getting Allied POWs home – 'Operation Exodus'.[183] This was based on airlifting POWs to advanced 'collection centres' at airfields near *Brussels* or *Reims* where they were 'encouraged' to bathe, get a haircut and don clean underclothes and fresh uniforms. Batches of men were then flown on across the channel (13,000 per day at the height of the exercise) to reception centres all over the south-east of England.

18
HOME AFTER FIVE LONG YEARS

Dad and Lloyd arrived back in England on Wednesday 23 May 1945. We don't know the exact departure point from eastern Germany nor journey details but they would have been counted off into a group of about 20–25 POWs and then loaded onto a Dakota or a shelled-out Lancaster bomber. Dad did once tell the family that they had been taken down low over the German town of *Essen* in order for them to see the devastation from RAF bombing raids, but he also said that he never wanted to fly again. Once on native soil, Dad was transferred to Reception Camp 93 for a few days where he was given decent food, plenty of tea and cigarettes and a comfortable bed. He was supplied with a leave pass, a ration card, some money, some cigarettes and a

Back home with the family – late May 1945. (Moonyé Checksfield).

*Lloyd in his fifties.
(Randall/Bird family).*

rail warrant. He would have been allowed one free telegram to his parents. He and Lloyd also completed the general questionnaire put to all returning Allied POWs.

Dad arrived home in *Woolaston* a couple of days later, over the weekend of 26/27 May 1945 (as, presumably, did Lloyd to *Woolstone*). Where possible, the family had gathered to welcome Dad home, knowing his arrival was imminent, a circumstance being replicated all over the country. His sister, Mary, had travelled over from Bristol with Eileen, her sister-in-law (and fiancée of Tom), to be with Dad's parents and younger brother, Tom. The bunting went up with a 'Welcome Home Ron' banner and Dad was suddenly spotted striding up 'Severn View', his home street. Someone later took a photograph to send to Ken, oldest brother, still serving in the Royal Navy. Though Dad had managed, somehow, to shed his uniform for the photograph, he was, technically, only on leave from the Army and returned to barracks on Monday 23 July.

The regimental authorities tried hard to persuade him to extend his army service and enticed him with promotion to Sergeant. It's no surprise that he refused, and he was discharged on Saturday 15 December 1945 having served, including his period as a POW, for 11 years.

Ron aged 60, about a year before his death.

He was, however, in the reserve for a further 14 years.* Fortunately, he was not called up for more service despite the Korean War, a conflict in which the Glosters played a significant part. He was lucky – many of his Regiment became POWs of the North Koreans/Chinese, and how

---

* Lloyd Randall also left the army after a few months – on 25 January 1946. He died of a heart attack on 14 May 1971.

Dad might or might not have coped with a second dose of captivity is a sobering train of thought.

Personally, I don't think he ever really recovered from the incarceration he actually suffered, certainly not enough to be able to talk about his experiences. In unearthing Dad's story from scraps of archive and by extrapolating from circumstantial evidence it has become more and more apparent why not.

Remembrance Sunday 2019

ACKNOWLEDGEMENTS

I WISH it were possible to give details of the many ways in which so many people have helped with this book, but it is not. However, before resorting to a mere list of names I must thank Elaine, my wife, specifically, for her support in researching the material and for her continuing forbearance. I may not have been listed as 'missing in action' as, once, was my father but I have often been 'missing' and antisocial. And I owe special thanks to our two sons. Both Alick and Huw have made substantial contributions and will, I hope, have been compensated in gleaning some knowledge of a grandfather they were never privileged to know. And then, in a list that bears no relation to priority I thank Jitka Strašilová, Jaroslav Strašil, Břetislav Zajíček, Tamara Zajíčková, Lenka Zajíčková, Anna Strašilová, Valerie Webb (née Beale), Melissa Atkinson, Moonyé Checksfield (née Beal), Joy Bird, Sarah Bird, Ann Randall, Curator of the Gloucestershire Regimental Museum Archive, Sebastian Mikulec of Centralne Muzeum Jeńców Wojennych, Lambinowice, Staff of The National Archive, Kew, Staff of The Army Personnel Centre, Glasgow, and Vendula Švábová of the Tourist Information Centre, Zábřeh. Finally, and further to the bare-bones list, I must thank John Chandler and the Hobnob Press. This exercise started as a scrapbook – just for the family – but John had the wisdom and enthusiasm to see that it could become a proper book for a general readership. He must have then regretted the work involved. The long 'heads down' sessions turning a 'pig's ear into a silk purse' deserve special credit and my sincere thanks.

November 2019

REFERENCES

1   Longden, Sean. *Hitler's British Slaves*. Arris Books, Moreton in Marsh 2005. p 9.

2   Full Military Service Record of 5182485 L/Cpl R A Beale, The Gloucestershire Regiment. Personal possession of author.

3   Allport, Alan. *Browned off and Bloody-minded: the British Soldier Goes to War*. Yale University Press, New Haven 2015. p 12.

4   Ibid. pp 21/22.

5   Smalley, Edward. *The British Expeditionary Force 1939 – 40*. Palgrave Macmillan, Basingstoke 2015. p 54.

6   Allport, Alan. *Browned off and Bloody-minded: the British Soldier Goes to War*. Yale University Press, New Haven 2015. pp 29-31.

7   Ibid. p 31.

8   Bruce, Colin John. *War on the Ground 1939 - 1945*. Constable, London 1995. p 27.

9   Allport, Alan. *Browned off and Bloody-minded: the British Soldier Goes to War*. Yale University Press, New Haven 2015. p 31.

10   Thompson, Julian. *Dunkirk, Retreat to Victory*. Sidgwick and Jackson, London 2008. p 6.

11   Fraser, David. *And we shall shock them. The British Army in the Second World War*. Hodder and Stoughton, London 1983. p 12.

12   Neitzel, Sonke and Welzer, Harald. *Soldaten*. Simon and Schuster, London 2012. p 35.

13   Aitken, Leslie. *Massacre on the road to Dunkirk*. Patrick Stephens, Wellingborough 1988. p 88.

14   Moorhouse, Roger. *First to fight. The Polish war 1939*. The Bodley Head, London 2019. pp 265/6.

15   Thompson, Julian. *Dunkirk, Retreat to Victory*. Sidgwick and Jackson, London 2008. pp 4/5.

16   Ibid. p 6.

17   Ibid. pp 5/6.

18   Fraser, David. *And we shall shock them. The British Army in the Second World War*. Hodder and Stoughton. London 1983. p 22.

19   Ibid. pp 22/23.

20   Smalley, Edward. *The British Expeditionary Force 1939 – 40*. Palgrave Macmillan, Basingstoke 2015. p 112.

21   Thompson, Julian. *Dunkirk, Retreat to Victory*. Sidgwick and Jackson, London 2008. p 13.

22   Smalley, Edward. *The British Expeditionary Force 1939 – 40*. Palgrave Macmillan, Basingstoke 2015. p 118.

23   Daniell, David Scott. *Cap of Honour. The Story of the Gloucestershire Regiment*. White Lion, London 1975. p 244.

24   Soldier's Pay Book (issued 6 June 1936) of 5182485 L/Cpl R A Beale, The Gloucestershire Regiment. Personal possession of author.

25   Sebag-Montefiore, Hugh. *Dunkirk, Fight to the Last Man*. Viking (Penguin), London 2006. pp 24/25.

26   Gilmore, E M B, Lt Col. Personal diary of the actions of Second Battalion Gloucestershire Regiment in France 1940. Gloucestershire Regimental Museum Archive, Gloucester. p 24.

27   Allport, Alan. *Browned off and Bloody-minded: the British Soldier Goes to War*. Yale University Press, New Haven 2015. pp 37/38.

28   Full Military Service Record of 5182485 L/Cpl R A Beale, The Gloucestershire Regiment. Personal possession of author.

29   Allport, Alan. *Browned off and Bloody-minded: the British Soldier Goes to War*. Yale University Press, New Haven 2015. p 44.

30   Spears, Edward. *Assignment to Catastophe, Volume 1 – Prelude to Dunkirk*. William Heinemann, London 1954. p 47 passim.

31   Thompson, Julian. *Dunkirk, retreat to victory*. Sidgwick and Jackson, London 2008. p 17.

32   Ibid.

33   Ibid, pp 36/ 37.

34   Sebag-Montefiore, Hugh. *Dunkirk, Fight to the Last Man*. Viking (Penguin), London 2006. p 26 passim.

35   Allport, Alan. *Browned off and Bloody-minded: the British Soldier Goes to War*. Yale University Press, New Haven 2015. p 44.

36   Daniell, David Scott. *Cap of Honour. The Story of the Gloucestershire Regiment*. White Lion, London 1975. p 244.

37   Ibid. p 245.

38   Ibid.

39   Sebag-Montefiore, Hugh. *Dunkirk, Fight to the Last Man*. Viking (Penguin), London 2006. p 46.

40   Daniell, David Scott. *Cap of Honour. The Story of the Gloucestershire Regiment*. White Lion, London 1975. p 248.

41   Sebag-Montefiore, Hugh. *Dunkirk, Fight to the Last Man*. Viking (Penguin), London 2006. p 80 passim.

42   Thompson, Julian. *Dunkirk, Retreat to Victory*. Sidgwick and Jackson, London 2008. p 40.

43   Smalley, Edward. *The British Expeditionary Force, 1939-40*. Palgrave Macmillan, Basingstoke 2015. p 27.

44   Paxman, Jeremy. *Great Britain's Great War*. Viking (Penguin), London 2013. p 77.

45   Ibid.

46   Wilson, H C W, Captain. Personal diary of the actions of Second Battalion Gloucestershire Regiment in France 1940. Gloucestershire Regimental Museum Archive, Gloucester. p 10.

47   Thompson, Julian. *Dunkirk, Retreat to Victory.* Sidgwick and Jackson, London 2008. p. 59.

48   Maddocks, Nick. *The West at War 1939 – 1945.* Sutton Publishing, Stroud 2005. pp 10/11.

49   Thompson, Julian. *Dunkirk, Retreat to Victory.* Sidgwick and Jackson, London 2008. p 59.

50   Daniell, David Scott. *Cap of Honour. The Story of the Gloucestershire Regiment.* White Lion, London 1975. p 251.

51   Maddocks, Nick. *The West at War 1939 – 1945.* Sutton Publishing, Stroud 2005. pp 11/12.

52   Thompson, Julian. *Dunkirk, Retreat to Victory.* Sidgwick and Jackson, London 2008. p 59.

53   Sebag-Montefiore, Hugh. *Dunkirk, Fight to the Last Man.* Viking (Penguin), London 2006. p 141.

54   Thompson, Julian. *Dunkirk, Retreat to Victory.* Sidgwick and Jackson, London 2008. p 83.

55   Neave, Airey. *The Flames of Calais.* Hodder and Stoughton, London 1972. p90.

56   Sebag-Montefiore, Hugh. *Dunkirk, Fight to the Last Man.* Viking (Penguin), London 2006. p 255.

57   Ibid. p 254.

58   Ibid. pp 255/256.

59   Ibid. p 249.

60   Ibid. p 246.

61   Ibid. p 257.

62   Ibid.

63   Ibid. p 258.

64   Ibid.

65   Maddocks, Nick. *The West at War 1939 – 1945.* Sutton Publishing, Stroud 2005. p 8.

66   Somerset N F, Brigadier, The Hon. Personal diary of the actions of 145 Brigade in France 1940. Gloucestershire Regimental Museum Archive, Gloucester. p 46.

67   Ibid. p 49.

68   Ibid. p 52.

69   https://www.cwgc.org/find-war-dead/casualty/2726329/cartland,-john-ronald-hamilton

70   Sebag-Montefiore, Hugh. *Dunkirk, Fight to the Last Man.* Viking (Penguin), London 2006. p 271.

71   Somerset N F, Brigadier, The Hon. Personal diary of the actions of 145 Brigade in France 1940. Gloucestershire Regimental Museum Archive, Gloucester. p 56.

72   Ibid. p 57.

73   Personal communication.
74   Somerset N F, Brigadier, The Hon. Personal diary of the actions of 145 Brigade in France 1940. Gloucestershire Regimental Museum Archive, Gloucester. p 57.
75   Ibid.
76   Maddocks, Nick. *The West at War 1939 – 1945*. Sutton Publishing, Stroud 2005. p 46.
77   Wilson, H C W, Captain. Personal diary of the actions of Second Battalion Gloucestershire Regiment in France 1940. Gloucestershire Regimental Museum Archive, Gloucester. p 15.
78   Maddocks, Nick. *The West at War 1939 – 1945*. Sutton Publishing, Stroud 2005. p 41.
79   Maddocks, Nick. *The West at War 1939 - 1945*. Sutton Publishing, Stroud 2005. p 42.
80   Wilson, H C W, Captain. Personal diary of the actions of Second Battalion Gloucestershire Regiment in France 1940. Gloucestershire Regimental Museum Archive, Gloucester. p 16.
81   Ibid. p 17.
82   Moorhouse, Roger. *First to Fight. The Polish War 1939*. The Bodley Head, London 2013. p 113.
83   Sebag-Montefiore, Hugh. *Dunkirk, Fight to the Last Man*. Viking (Penguin), London 2006. p 299.
84   Aitken, Leslie. *Massacre on the Road to Dunkirk. Wormhout 1940*. Patrick Stephens, Wellingborough 1988. pp 86 – 94.
85   Maddocks, Nick. *The West at War 1939 – 1945*. Sutton Publishing, Stroud 2005. p 42.
86   Daniell, David Scott. *Cap of Honour. The Story of the Gloucestershire Regiment*. White Lion, London 1975. p 261.
87   Full military service record of 5182485 R A Beale. Personal possession of author.
88   Ibid.
89   Longden, Sean. *Dunkirk, the Men they Left Behind*. Constable, London 2008. p 263.
90   Ibid. p 268.
91   Ibid. p 269.
92   Mackenzie, S. P. *The Colditz Myth*. OUP, Oxford 2004. p 70.
93   Longden, Sean. *Dunkirk, the Men they Left Behind*. Constable, London 2008. p 269.
94   Rolf, David. *Prisoners of the Reich*. Coronet Books, Sevenoaks 1989. p 30.
95   Makepeace, Clare. *Captives of War. British Prisoners of War in Europe in the Second World War*. Cambridge University Press, Cambridge 2017. p 148.
96   Waite, Charles (with La Vardera, Dee). *Survivor of the Long March*. The History Press, Stroud 2010. p 63.
97   Longden, Sean. *Dunkirk, the Men they Left Behind*. Constable, London 2008. p 311.

98   Waite, Charles (with La Vardera, Dee). *Survivor of the Long March*. The History Press, Stroud 2010. pp 63/64.

99   Ibid. p 65.

100   Ibid. p 66.

101   Evans, Arthur. *Sojourn in Silesia*. Ashford Writers, Ashford, Kent 2000. p 16.

102   Ibid.

103   Ibid.

104   Wickiewicz, Anna. *Captivity in British Uniforms, Stalag VIIIB (344), Lamsdorf*. Centralne Muzeum Jeńców Wojennych, Opole, Poland 2018. p 9.

105   Evans, Arthur. *Sojourn in Silesia*. Ashford Writers, Ashford, Kent 2000. p 16.

106   Ibid. p 17.

107   Longden, Sean. *Hitler's British Slaves*. Arris Books, Moreton in Marsh 2005. p 134.

108   Evans, Arthur. *Sojourn in Silesia*. Ashford Writers, Ashford, Kent 2000. p 18.

109   Rolf, David. *Prisoners of the Reich*. Coronet Books, Sevenoaks 1989. p 64.

110   Edgar, Donald. *The Stalag Men*. John Clare, London 1982. p 73.

111   Longden, Sean. *Hitler's British Slaves*. Arris Books, Moreton in Marsh 2005. Preface.

112   Ibid.

113   Rolf, David. *Prisoners of the Reich*. Coronet Books, Sevenoaks 1989. p 98.

114   German record card of work history of POW 10582 R A Beale. Personal possession of author.

115   Rolf, David. *Prisoners of the Reich*. Coronet Books, Sevenoaks 1989. p 78.

116   Ibid. p 80.

117   Mackenzie, S. P. *The Colditz Myth*. OUP, Oxford 2004. p 160.

118   Longden, Sean. *Hitler's British Slaves*. Arris Books, Moreton in Marsh 2005. p 37.

119   Ibid. p 147.

120   Edgar, Donald. *The Stalag Men*. John Clare, London 1982. p 58.

121   German record card of work history of POW 10582 R A Beale. Personal possession of author.

122   Guttridge, Tom. *Behind the Wire*. Amberley, Stroud, Gloucestershire 2017. p 66.

123   Ibid. pp 66-68.

124   Mackenzie, S. P. *The Colditz Myth*. OUP, Oxford 2004. p 195.

125   Ibid. pp 195/196.

126   German record card of medical history of POW 10582 R A Beale. Personal possession of author.

127   Ibid.

128   Ibid.

129   Rolf, David. *Prisoners of the Reich*. Coronet Books, Sevenoaks 1989. p 112.

130   German record card of work history of POW 10582 R A Beale. Personal possession of author.

131   Rolf, David. *Prisoners of the Reich*. Coronet Books, Sevenoaks 1989. p 94.
132   Longden, Sean. *Hitler's British Slaves*. Arris Books, Moreton in Marsh 2005. pp 194/195.
133   Rolf, David. *Prisoners of the Reich*. Coronet Books, Sevenoaks 1989. p 126.
134   Longden, Sean. *Hitler's British Slaves*. Arris Books, Moreton in Marsh 2005. p 39.
135   Edgar, Donald. *The Stalag Men*. John Clare, London 1982. p 140.
136   Rolf, David. *Prisoners of the Reich*. Coronet Books, Sevenoaks 1989. p 139.
137   Edgar, Donald. *The Stalag Men*. John Clare, London 1982. p 105.
138   https://en.wikipedia.org › wiki › Stalag_VIII-F
139   Little, Duncan. *Allies in Auschwitz*. Clairview, Forest Row, East Sussex 2009. p 2.
140   Longden, Sean. *Hitler's British Slaves*. Arris Books, Moreton in Marsh 2005. p 85.
141   Little, Duncan. *Allies in Auschwitz*. Clairview, Forest Row, East Sussex 2009. p 18.
142   Ibid. p 29.
143   German record card of work history of POW 10582 R A Beale. Personal possession of author.
144   https://en.wikipedia.org › wiki › *Blechhammer*.
145   German record card of work history of POW 10582 R A Beale. Personal possession of author.
146   German record card of medical history of POW 10582 R A Beale. Personal possession of author.
147   German record card of work history of POW 10582 R A Beale. Personal possession of author.
148   Ibid.
149   The National Archives, Kew. Liberated Prisoner of War Interrogation Questionnaires, WO 344: form completed by 5182485 Lance Corporal R A Beale.
150   Keegan, John. *The Second World War*. Hutchinson. London 1989. p 40.
151   Ibid. p 488.
152   Trueman. C N. "*Czechoslovakia resistance*" historylearningsite.co.uk. Aug 2016.
153   Longden, Sean. *Hitler's British Slaves*. Arris Books, Moreton in Marsh 2005. p 122.
154   Ibid. p 180.
155   Ibid. p 178.
156   Edgar, Donald. *The Stalag Men*. John Clare, London 1982. p 140.
157   Longden, Sean. *Hitler's British Slaves*. Arris Books, Moreton in Marsh 2005. p 190.
158   Ibid. p 173.
159   Ibid. p 128.
160   MacDonald, Charles B. *The Last Offensive*. Centre of Military History, Washington D C, USA 1993. p 9.
161   Hastings, Max. *All Hell Let Loose*. Harper Press, London 2011. p 611.

162   Mackenzie, S. P. *The Colditz Myth*. OUP, Oxford 2004. p 358.

163   Keegan, John. *The Second World War*. Hutchinson. London 1989. p 519.

164   MacDonald, Charles B. *The Last Offensive*. Centre of Military History, Washington D C, USA 1993. p 381 Passim.

165   Ibid. p 378.

166   Ibid. p 454.

167   Evans, Arthur. *Sojourn in Silesia*. Ashford Writers, Ashford, Kent 2000. pp 79/80.

168   Longden, Sean. *Hitler's British Slaves*. Arris Books, Moreton in Marsh 2005. p 204.

169   Nichol, John; Rennell Tony. *The Last Escape*. Penguin, London 2002. p 151.

170   https://www.sciencespo.fr/mass-violence-war-massacre-resistance/en/document/*nazi-death-marches*-1944-1945.

171   Ibid.

172   Nichol, John; Rennell Tony. *The Last Escape*. Penguin, London 2002. p 136.

173   Ibid. p 170.

174   German record card of work history of POW 10582 R A Beale. Personal possession of author.

175   https://en.wikipedia.org › wiki › Gliwice.

176   Clutton-Brook, Oliver. *Footprints on the sands of time. RAF Bomber Command Prisoners of War in Germany 1939 – 45*. Grub Street, London 2003. p 38.

177   Full military service record of 5182445 Cpl F L Randall, The Gloucestershire Regiment. Personal possession of author. Passim.

178   The National Archives, Kew. Liberated Prisoner of War Interrogation Questionnaires, WO 344: form completed by 5182445 Corporal F L Randall.

179   Johnson, Tony. *Escape to Freedom*. Leo Cooper, Barnsley 2002. pp 151/152.

180   Hackett, John, General Sir, *I was a Stranger*. Sphere Books, London 1979. pp 87/88.

181   MacDonald, Charles B. *The Last Offensive*. Centre of Military History, Washington D C, USA 1993. p 425.

182   The National Archives, Kew. Liberated Prisoner of War Interrogation Questionnaires, WO 344: form completed by 5182445 Corporal F L Randall.

183   Nichol, John; Rennell Tony. *The Last Escape*. Penguin, London 2002. p 341.

INDEX